The Story Underlying the Numbers

The Story Underlying the Numbers

*A Simple Approach
to Comprehensive Financial
Statements Analysis*

S. Veena Iyer

 BUSINESS EXPERT PRESS

The Story Underlying the Numbers: A Simple Approach to Comprehensive Financial Statements Analysis
Copyright © Business Expert Press, LLC, 2018.

First published in 2018 by
Business Expert Press, LLC
222 East 46th Street, New York, NY 10017
www.businessexpertpress.com

ISBN-13: 978-1-94784-376-9 (paperback)
ISBN-13: 978-1-94784-377-6 (e-book)

Business Expert Press Financial Accounting and Auditing Collection

Collection ISSN: 2151-2795 (print)
Collection ISSN: 2151-2817 (electronic)

Cover and interior design by S4Carlisle Publishing Services
Private Ltd., Chennai, India

First edition: 2018

10 9 8 7 6 5 4 3 2 1

Printed in the United States of America.

Dedication

To my parents

Abstract

Very often it is observed that when faced with financial statements of a firm, students and even practitioners are at a loss as to where to begin the analysis. Most simply compute every ratio they know and interpret them in a standalone manner. They are unable to thread them together to spin a meaningful story that can completely or at least substantially explain what might be probably happening in the firm. Unless the individual studying the financial statements—whether an investor, management personnel, third-party analyst, or any other party of interest—is able to identify underlying issues and come up with probable causes, decision making with regard to investment or pulling out, or with regard to resolving the problem, will remain flawed. This book is aimed at students and working executives who have a rudimentary prior understanding of the three primary financial statements—the balance sheet, the income statement, and the cash flow statement—as well as familiarity with the very basic financial ratios. The book uses a logical, top-down approach to unraveling the underlying story of the firm. If you are an executive at a firm in a decision-making capacity, this book is for you. It is a myth that only executives in the finance function need to understand financial statements. Every decision within a firm has implications for the financial statements and the need for such knowledge increases as one goes up the corporate ladder. The book is intended to be free flowing, with minimum jargon so as to be understood and appreciated especially by nonfinance executives and students of business and management.

Keywords

Du-Pont framework, financial ratios, financial statements analysis, performance analysis

Contents

Acknowledgments

First and foremost, I thank all the corporate executives who have participated in Executive Development Programmes at MDI Gurgaon over the years and helped me hone and enhance the Du-Pont analysis version used in this book. Their appreciation for the insight gained from the analysis and encouragement to pen a book plugging this gap has been instrumental in my decision to pick up this topic.

I thank my colleagues at MDI Gurgaon who already have publications with BEP as that provided me the confidence and drive to try out this book. I cannot thank my colleagues and friends enough who have been encouraging me through the journey to keep it going.

My family—my husband, my daughters, my parents, and my perpetual fan, my sister! Your encouragement and constant support has given me the confidence and made it possible for me to pen this book down within the tight timelines I set for myself. I could not have done this without you.

I take this opportunity to thank Mark Bettner for his incisive review, and Scott Isenberg and the entire BEP team for giving me this opportunity and helping me at every step of the way to bring this effort to fruition.

Last but not least, the supreme power up there, without whose divine will nothing is possible.

CHAPTER 1

Why Financial Statements Analysis?

Financial statements are a firm's or any business's report card. They summarize the performance of the firm over a specified prior period mainly using quantitative metrics, supplemented by qualitative reporting. Just as a child gets her report card at the end of a term or year, a firm produces its report card for the benefit of those who have a stake in its performance and future. Just as a child's report card becomes a useless piece of document unless the parent analyzes the information to understand what has gone right and wrong during the year and what steps can be taken to rectify mistakes and improve performance, financial statements of a firm can become meaningless documents unless the management and more importantly, its stakeholders analyze it to understand the story beneath.

The financial statements are (a) the report card of a firm's performance, (b) symptoms of underlying issues, and (c) portents for the future. These statements are the means to unravel the story, not an end in themselves. They contain a wealth of information—both expressed and implied—and it is up to the stakeholders to utilize this information to the best of their ability for better decision making.

Smart financial statements analysis requires a good understanding of the terminology and design of the financial statements, of tools used for financial statements analysis, and of the business of the firm itself. Many students of business and even people in practice mistake financial statements analysis for simply computing financial ratios and stating obvious observations. Ratios are an essential tool no doubt, but blindly computing those to arrive at standalone observations, which are in turn mistaken for conclusions, can be dangerous.

Objectives of a Firm

Theory of the firm is almost as old as the discipline of economics itself. Ronald Coase, in his celebrated work, *The Nature of the Firm* (1937), explained that firms are set up by people in response to the limitations of the price mechanism to independently direct production, consumption, and prices in an economy. Price mechanism presumes the parties to an exchange to enter into explicit or implicit complete contracts each time an exchange happens. This is impractical and infeasible as the time, effort, and monetary cost of such contracting will far exceed the benefits of the exchange. However, when such exchanges are patterned together within firms, contracts need to be written only among firms and not individuals. Firms have the ability to draw up longer term contracts, albeit incomplete, with various parties at the same time at a reduced cost and enable exchanges and transactions to take place.

Alchian and Demsetz (1972) emphasized the benefit of teamwork that firms allow. The benefits of this teamwork extend to acquisition of resources as well, both physical and monetary. A corporation is able to raise financial capital from a multitude of small investors who chip in small portions and get the additional benefit of limited liability. The organizational setup of the firm further enables a few elected representatives to take decisions on behalf of all investors in the corporation that significantly reduces transaction costs and time and improves efficiency. It is implied in this setup that the management has a fiduciary responsibility to all the stakeholders of the firm and particularly to the equity holders, to keep their interest paramount in all decision making. This is beautifully elucidated by Jensen and Meckling in their seminal work on agency theory.

The corporate finance discipline defines the primary role of the firm as run by its management, overseen by the board of directors to be maximization of returns for its shareholders. Over time this definition has undergone change to become more inclusive and less materialistic. A firm exists for and thrives because of stakeholders that include the state, the society, and the public at large. Firms have to now look at delivering on a triple bottom-line rather than a single bottom-line. The triple bottom-line includes environmental sustainability and corporate social responsibility besides shareholder returns.

Financial statements analysis is all about measuring and assessing the firm's performance on the financial returns metrics, assuming the firm is playing its part in being a good citizen. In fact, being a good citizen is not considered a cost that takes away from financial profits or returns. On the contrary, firms see a positive spillover of adopting a responsible attitude toward the environment and society at large on their business and financial metrics. Stakeholders, over time, have become more discerning and sensitive to businesses' contribution, positive or negative, to the social fabric and environment. They accordingly, reward or penalize firms that finally has an impact on the latter's financial metrics. Recently, there was a debate in the Indian financial media whether the Life Insurance Corporation of India (LIC), the largest domestic institutional investor should pull out its equity investment from ITC Ltd., the largest tobacco product manufacturer in the country. It was a debate between LIC's responsibility toward its investors versus toward society.

Activities-of-a-Firm Approach to Financial Statements Analysis

Having understood the rationale for why a firm comes into being and its responsibilities toward its various stakeholders, we turn our attention to how the firm can be understood for the purposes of financial statements analysis. A firm is a complex being. It can be studied and its design and structure can be analyzed and evaluated from various perspectives. Some of the most popular ones include the industrial economics, organization design, portfolio of products or businesses perspectives. However, for our purposes, we look at a firm as the combination of three activities— operational, investment, and financing activities.

Any firm, however complex, can classify each of its activities into one of these three categories. In fact, that is the premise of the cash flow statement, one of the key financial statements published by firms. A firm comes into being with an idea of providing products or services to a set of potential customers, through a unique value proposition. How to provide the product/ service determines the operating activities of the firm. Once that is decided, the firm needs to plan what kind of a setup it needs in place to be able to operate. This determines its investment activities.

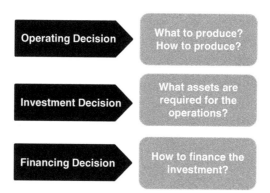

Figure 1.1 The activities of a firm

Once that is decided, the firm needs to plan the quantum of funds it needs and the sources it will tap. This determines its financing activities. Figure 1.1 portrays this logical connect between operating, investment and financing decisions of a firm.

This is a simple idea of how a business starts and comes into being. Once a business establishes itself and grows, these activities continue over its lifetime. The firm has to keep making investments in order to grow, continue operating efficiently in order to earn profits, and finally, source funds either internally or externally in order to keep the ball rolling. We use this framework to understand and analyze its financial statements.

The Principal Financial Statements

There are four[1] essential financial statements drawn up by firms under Ind-AS—the set of rules Indian companies have to adhere to while drawing up their financial statements—especially those that are listed on the stock exchanges. These are the Balance Sheet as at the end of the accounting period (also called the Statement of Financial Position), the Profit and Loss statement for the period (also called the

---

[1]There are slight variations in the presentation mandated by different bodies governing accounting standards and rules. The U.S. GAAP requires firms to draw up five statements; a statement of comprehensive earnings besides the four mentioned here. Under Ind-AS, contents of this statement are subsumed in the statement of change in equity.

Income Statement), the Cash Flow Statement for the period, and the Statement of changes in equity for the period.

Formats of financial statements in each country are dictated by the laws of the land, specifically the regulatory authorities that decide on accounting conventions and those that may be regulating the sector itself. In India, the accounting regulations are governed by the Ministry of Corporate Affairs and the Institute of Chartered Accountants of India. The Ind-AS are designed on the IFRS[2] conventions.

The balance sheet provides a summary of the financial position of a firm as on a particular date; what the firm owns (assets) and what it owes (liabilities). Any firm essentially sources funds from two main sources—owners and lenders—to invest in assets. These funds are called shareholder equity and debt funds (or inside and outside liabilities), respectively. At the beginning of the life of a firm, therefore, the total book value of its assets is equal to the total book value of its shareholder funds and outside liabilities. This is famously known as the accounting equation or accounting identity and forms the basis for all financial accounting, the world over.

At the inception of a firm, Assets = Shareholder equity + Outside liabilities.

This relationship is sacrosanct and ensures that the balance sheet is always balanced. Figure 1.2 lays out the essential components of a typical balance sheet. The layout does not specifically follow any convention such as U.S. GAAP or IFRS but is meant to simply illustrate the accounting identity and the components of a standard balance sheet.

As the firm begins its operations, it earns revenues and incurs expenses. These get recorded in the profit and loss statement (hereafter referred to

---

[2]IFRS stands for International Financial Reporting Standards toward which global accounting practices are converging. With almost all European countries already following IFRS, others such as India and even the U.S. (which developed and still follows the U.S. GAAP) are moving in that direction in the interest of common global standards. India's erstwhile accounting standards IAS have been modified to resemble IFRS to a great extent under the Ind-AS standards. While nonfinancial listed firms were to have transitioned to Ind-AS by FY2017 (subject to conditions), financial firms are to transition to it in phases starting 1st April, 2018.

Shareholder equity and liabilities	Assets
A.1.Share capital	D.1.Tangible assets
A.2.Reserves and surpluses	D.2.Intangible assets
A.Shareholder equity	D.3.Other noncurrent assets
	D.Total noncurrent assets
B.1.Long term loans and borrowing	
B.2.Other long-term liabilities	E.1.Cash and cash equivalents
B.Total noncurrent liabilities	E.2.Investments
	E.3.Trade receivables
C.1.Trade payables	E.4.Inventory
C.2.Short term loans and advances	E.5.Other current assets
C.3.Provisions	E. Total current assets
C.Total current liabilities	
Total liabilities and shareholder equity (A + B + C)	Total Assets (D + E)
$A + B + C = D + E$	

Figure 1.2 Layout of a balance sheet

Revenues from operations
Less: Cost of sales
= Gross profit
Less: Other operating expenses
= Cash operating profit (EBITDA)
Less: Depreciation and amortization charges
= Operating profit (EBIT)
Add: Other income
Less: Interest expenses
= Profits before taxes (PBT)
Less: Provision for taxes
= Profits after tax (PAT, also called Net Income)

Figure 1.3 Layout of the P&L statement

Notes: EBITDA stands for Earnings before interest, taxes, depreciation, and amortization; EBIT stands for Earnings before interest and taxes. Depreciation and amortization are estimates of the extent of usage of tangible and intangible assets respectively during the accounting period.

as P&L) and at the end of a period, the P&L shows the profit or loss the firm's operations have earned as illustrated in Figure 1.3.

The net income is the residual left after all the stakeholders have been paid their dues and this belongs to the shareholders (owners). If this is a profit, it enhances their equity and if the firm's operations result in losses, they erode the owner's equity. Therefore, once a firm begins operations,

Profits before taxes (from P&L statement) Remove: Effect of nonoperating items in the P&L Remove: Effect of noncash items in the P&L (+/−) Changes in working capital items (current assets and current liability items in the balance sheet) (−):cash outflow on payment of income taxes = **Cash flows from operating activities (A)**
(+/−) net cash flows from sale/purchase of long-term operating assets (+/−) net cash flows from sale/purchase of investments = **Cash flows from investment activities (B)**
(+) cash inflows from equity or long-term debt issues (−) cash outflows from repayment of debt/ buyback of stock (−) cash outflows from interest payments on debt (−) cash outflows from dividend payments = **Cash flows from financing activities (C)**
A + B + C = Net cash flows during the period (D)
Opening balance of cash and cash equivalents + D = Closing balance of cash and cash equivalents

Figure 1.4 Layout of the cash flow statement

shareholder equity becomes an output of the accounting equation rather than an input.[3] The accounting equation now becomes:

$$\text{Shareholder equity} = \text{Assets} - \text{Outside Liabilities}$$

The statement of cash flows (hereafter referred to as CFS) lays out the inflows and outflows of cash into and from the firm over an accounting period, categorized into the three activity buckets defined earlier in Figure 1.1. The net cash inflow or outflow during the period is added to the cash balance at the beginning of the period to give the ending balance of cash for the period as presented in Figure 1.4.

---

[3]There are also gains and losses that accrue to shareholders that do not get reflected in the P& L. These make their way into shareholder equity through the statement of changes in other comprehensive earnings or income (OCI), mentioned in an earlier footnote. Some such sources of other comprehensive incomes are unrealized gains and losses when tradable investments in the balance sheet are "marked-to-market." This is explained in greater detail in Chapters 5 and 6 while discussing financial services. When noncurrent assets and liabilities are revalued to their fair values, the resulting increase or decrease in their values results in changes in the OCI for shareholders.

To the extent the elements in the balance sheet and P&L have cash implications, they find a place in the CFS. For example if the firm purchases an asset on credit, there would be no cash implication and it will not affect the cash flow statement. However, in the interest of information and true reporting, the firm may record the purchase of asset as a cash outflow from investment activity and the corresponding credit taken as a cash inflow from financing activity. This shows that financial statements are more than mere final tallies; their essential function is true and fair presentation of the activities and goings-on of a business.

We summarize the key characteristics of the three financial statements discussed so far in Figure 1.5.

Since the P&L and CFS pertain to specific periods of time, they are started afresh at the beginning of each period and closed out at the end of the period. They explain *what has happened during a period*, which is why they are *flow statements*. On the other hand, since the balance sheet informs about the financial position of the firm *as at a point in time*, it is a *cumulative statement*. The balance sheet at the end of a period is nothing but the balance sheet at the beginning of the period to which the effect of the "flows" from the P&L and CFS pertaining to the period is added. Therefore, a balance sheet is a *stock statement*.

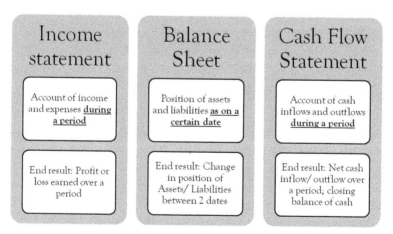

Figure 1.5 The principal financial statements

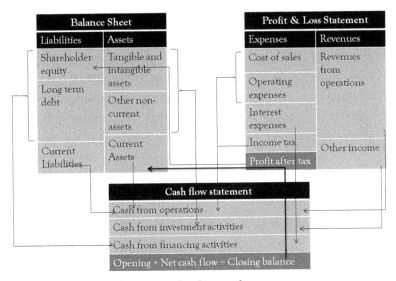

Figure 1.6 Interlinks among the financial statements

The reader might wonder as to the difference between the P&L and the CFS. Is the profit or loss earned not the same as net cash surplus or deficit during the period? It would be, if the firm were following *cash-based accounting*. In this system, revenues are recognized when received and expenses are recognized when paid. Therefore, there would be no difference between the P&L and CFS. However, firms world over (except specific entities such as not-for-profit organizations) follow the *accrual system of accounting* for profit or loss. This requires revenues to be recognized when they are earned and expenses to be recognized when they fall due or accrue.

The accrual system results in recognition of revenues not received and expenses not paid as also cash received or paid in advance or in arrears in relation to the recognition of revenues and expenses. These in turn, give rise to assets and liabilities in the form of money owed to or owed by the firm to third parties, besides the assets and liabilities the firm starts its life with.

The P&L, balance sheet and CFS are interconnected statements and work like a jigsaw puzzle where each element neatly fits in order for the accounting identity to hold. This dovetailing of the three statements can be understood from Figure 1.6.

Financial statements are more than attaching numbers to assets, liabilities, revenues, and expenses, and putting them all together to arrive at profit or loss or total assets or liabilities. Their presentation is as important as their content as we will see in the following chapters. Classification and presentation of transactions, items, and metrics can significantly change the meaning that is conveyed. This makes understanding financial statements and deciphering them an exciting as well as a challenging task.

CHAPTER 2

Introducing the Core Framework

Being a complex organism, getting even a reasonable grip on what goes on inside a corporation spanning businesses and geographies simply from its financial statements is indeed a tall order. An analyst or any other interested party who has to make do with publicly available information has to supplement the information in the financial statements with the wealth of qualitative and quantitative information available in the corporation's annual reports, corporate website, media reports, etc. in order to claim that she has understood the underlying scenario fairly well. However, the financial statements are a starting point, and a very important one at that. They provide the nucleus of the story and unless we get that right, the layers that will be built using other information will be flawed and meaningless or at the least, present an incorrect picture of the firm.

Across the world, publicly listed firms have to mandatorily publish their annual and quarterly reports for the benefit of their stakeholders. Of the four (or five) financial statements mandated by accounting standard setting bodies across the world, in this book, we shall focus primarily on the first three statements, namely, the P&L statement, the balance sheet, and the cash flow statement.

Any textbook of financial accounting or financial statements analysis begins with the basic tools.

1. A common-size analysis of the financial statements requires expressing each item of the balance sheet and P&L statement as a percentage of the balance sheet total and gross revenue, respectively. This is compared across years to study how individual items have moved as a proportion of the total.

2. A time series analysis requires indexing each item of the balance sheet and P&L to the corresponding item of a base year to examine movement and growth of each item over time.

3. The third and one of the most commonly used tools is financial ratios. A simple yet powerful tool, financial ratios are well understood across the business and analyst community. While some are understood almost similarly, many are flexible and can be defined to suit a context. Besides, suitable ratios can be designed by the user studying specific business problems. The only caveats with ratio analysis are consistency of definition and measurement and proper interpretation for decision making.

In this book, we use financial ratios as the core of our framework. Most financial ratios use information from the balance sheet and P&L statements. The cash flow statement (CFS) gets neglected most of the time and the wealth of information it contains is thereby wasted. We shall describe how the CFS can be tied to our financial ratios based framework and finally, what kind of other information can be used in order to substantiate and strengthen inferences drawn from the financial statements analysis.

The DuPont Analysis Approach

The DuPont analysis framework[1] is a simple yet powerful tool to analyze the financial performance of a firm. Its starting point is the premise that as the contributors of risk capital and recipients of residual profits and assets, the maximization of returns to equity holders is the ultimate objective of a firm. Hence, the return on equity (ROE), also referred to as return on net worth (RONW), is the starting point.

ROE = Profits after tax (PAT)/Average shareholder equity (Equity) (1)

Before going any further with the framework, it is necessary to understand why ROE (or RONW) is the core ratio equity investors

---

[1]This framework gets its name from the DuPont Corporation that first used it in the 1920s.

should be interested in. Anyone investing in the equity of a firm receives returns in the form of dividends and capital gains. Very simply put, a firm can distribute dividends only if it is earning healthy profits (and sufficiently in cash!) and has surplus leftover after retaining a portion of such profits for its reinvestment needs. As we will see later, this is also defined as the firm's free cash flows. A firm's share price is an increasing function of its expected future free cash flows and a decreasing function of the riskiness of these cash flows. So whether the returns are in the form of dividends or capital gains, the firm needs to have an expected stream of healthy and growing free cash flows.

Where do these cash flows arise from? Their primary source is operating profits. And how are operating profits generated? Operating profits is what is left over from revenues after all expenses have been paid. Revenues, in turn, are generated by putting operating assets into use. A firm's operating assets are acquired by funds contributed by equity holders and debt-holders (lenders). Free cash flows accruing to each of these stakeholders will be a function of their share of funds invested into the firm's assets and returns generated on this investment *that are passed on to the stakeholder group*. For lenders, this translates into debt capital invested into assets and rate of interest charged on such capital. For equity holders, this translates into equity capital invested into assets and ROE earned on such equity.[2] Therefore, the ROE is a key determinant of the share price of a firm and an indicator of whether shareholder funds are being invested wisely.

Equation (1) can be expanded into three key components as follows.

$$\text{ROE} = (\text{PAT/Revenues}) \times (\text{Revenues/Average total assets [Assets]})$$
$$\times (\text{Assets/Equity})$$

$$= \text{Net profits margin (NPM)} \times \text{Asset turnover ratio (ATR)}$$
$$\times \text{Financial leverage (LEV)} \qquad (2)$$

---

[2]For a firm making sufficient profits, lenders' returns are restricted to the interest charged on debt held by them while equity-holders' returns comprise all residual profits, measured by ROE. Maximizing ROE by bringing in fixed-return funding such as debt is termed as Trading on Equity.

This is the commonly used formulation of the DuPont analysis. Let us term this the 3-way DuPont framework. It clearly expresses the ROE as a function of the firm's profitability, asset utilization and financial leverage. Seen from our activities-of-a-firm perspective, the three components are nothing but an outcome of the firm's operating, investing, and financial activities, respectively, as depicted in Figure 2.1. The three ratios are a measure of how well a firm is managing its operations that includes revenue generation, pricing, and cost controls; how well the firm is utilizing its assets to generate revenues that includes a firm's decision regarding which assets to be acquired, to buy, or to rent and the depreciation policy; and finally, how the firm decides to finance these assets using owned and loaned funds, respectively.

On comparing ROE of a firm with a peer or with the same firm's ROE for prior periods, any improvement or drop in ROE can be further investigated by examining the movement across the three components. This helps in zeroing in on the problem area (or an area where significant improvement has been seen) and investigating it further.

But before we move on to isolate one of the three components for further analysis, it is important to understand what the DuPont formulation implies. Prima facie it says that ROE can be maximized by improving either one or more of the three components; and that includes financial leverage. In other words, increasing debt in the capital structure improves ROE! But that sounds counterintuitive. So where's the bug?

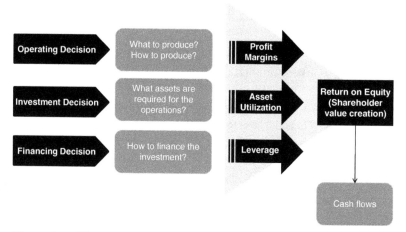

Figure 2.1 The 3-way DuPont framework

The 4-Way and 5-Way DuPont Frameworks

Financial leverage clearly improves ROE, but subject to conditions. Financial leverage means more debt and more debt means more interest charges. This automatically hits at the net profit margin (NPM). It is clearly not a ceteris paribus[3] situation. So does an increase in LEV lead to a proportionate reduction in NPM so as to nullify the impact on ROE? This requires further understanding of this relationship that can provide very powerful insights to management, lenders, and analysts who take decisions regarding capital structure, lending, and investing.

We break down Equation (2) into further components to come up with a 5-way DuPont model.

$$\begin{aligned} \text{ROE} = [&(\text{PAT/Profits before taxes (PBT)}) \\ &\times (\text{PBT/Earnings before interest and taxes (EBIT)}) \\ &\times (\text{EBIT/Revenues})] \times (\text{Revenues/Assets}) \\ &\times (\text{Assets/Equity}) \end{aligned} \qquad (3)$$

This framework breaks NPM down into three components that bring out the effect of income tax liability, interest expenses, and operating margins separately. Looking at it another way, the third term indicates the proportion of revenues remaining after all 'operational lenders' have been paid, which include suppliers and employees. The second term indicates the proportion of operating profit that remains after financial lenders have been paid their due and the first term indicates the proportion of profits that remain after the state has been paid its share in the form of taxes. This is an easily understood formulation that helps a lay person quickly get a grip on how the revenues generated by the firm are distributed across stakeholders who contribute to the earning of that revenue and hence, what is left for the equity holders. Figure 2.2 expresses the components of the Income Statement as returns to various stakeholders. This is an intuitive yet powerful way to dismantle a firm's activities according to decision types involving different stakeholders.

The 5-way DuPont is not a very elegant exposition from a decision-making perspective. So we will conduct some simple mathematical manipulation on Equation (3) to come up with a more meaningful

---

[3]Ceteris paribus is a Latin term that means "holding all else constant." This is commonly used in framing and understanding theories and principles in economics.

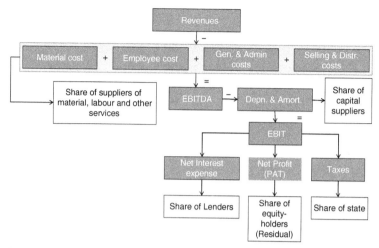

Figure 2.2 The P&L statement as share of stakeholders on revenues generated

and useful formulation. We expand some of the terms in the equation to come up with the following:

$$\text{ROE} = [\text{PBT}\,(1 - t)/\text{PBT}] \times [(\text{EBIT} - \text{Interest})/\text{EBIT}]$$
$$\times [\text{EBIT/Revenue}] \times [\text{Revenue/Assets}]$$
$$\times [\text{Assets/ Equity}]$$

where "t" stands for the income tax rate applicable to the firm.

$$= [1 - t] \times [1 - (\text{Int/EBIT})] \times [\text{EBIT/Revenue}]$$
$$\times [\text{Revenue/Assets}] \times [\text{Assets/Equity}]$$

Combining the first and the third terms in the expression, we get,

$$= [(1 - (\text{Int/EBIT})] \times [\text{EBIT}(1 - t)/\text{Revenue}]$$
$$\times [\text{Revenue/Assets}] \times [\text{Assets/Equity}]$$

$$= [(1 - (1/\text{ICR})] \times [\text{NOPAT/Revenue}]$$
$$\times [\text{Revenue/Assets}] \times [\text{Assets/Equity}] \quad\quad (4)$$

where, ICR is the interest coverage ratio measured as EBIT divided by interest expense and NOPAT[4] is the 'net operating profit after tax' measured as EBIT$(1 - t)$.

---

[4]NOPAT is also sometimes referred to as EBIAT - Earnings before interest but after tax.

ICR measures the number of times a firm's operating profit can "cover" its interest liability for the year. Higher a firm's ICR, greater is its resilience with respect to financial distress arising on account of debt in its capital structure.

ROE is now expressed as a product of four terms,[5] of which the last two terms are the same as earlier, that is, ATR and LEV. The NPM that measures profitability has been broken down into two components that represent the financial part and operational part of the NPM, respectively. The second term NOPAT/Revenue is nothing but the posttax operating margin of the firm. The first term of the equation is a function of the ICR and higher the ICR, higher will be this term and hence, greater will ROE be. Let us call this term *financial resilience* (RES). So how does financial leverage really impact ROE?

Let us rewrite Equation (4) by combining the second and the third terms thus:

$$ROE = [1 - (1/ICR)] \times [(NOPAT/Revenue) \times (Revenue/Assets)] \times [Assets/Equity]$$

$$ROE = [1 - (1/ICR)] \times [NOPAT^6/Assets] \times [Assets/Equity]$$

$$ROE = RES \times Return\ on\ assets\ (ROA)^7 \times LEV \qquad (5)$$

---

[5]Elements that have been ignored in this derivation but can be a non-trivial component for some firms are Other Income and Exceptional Items. In this derivation we have assumed either zero or negligible amount of these variables that can be loaded into EBIT without affecting our analysis materially. However, if other income is a considerable proportion of a firm's total revenue or either of the terms has the effect of turning a loss situation profitable, it needs to be analyzed separately. We shall look at such instances in subsequent chapters.

[6]The reader should observe that this relationship holds even in a situation where the income tax rate is zero. Certain countries have near-zero or zero income tax on corporate profits or particular industries or businesses may enjoy tax holiday by the government. In such cases, NOPAT = EBIT.

[7]Very often ROA is computed as PAT/Average total assets. This is an inconsistent and incorrect measure. Both lenders and equity holders have claims on the total assets of a firm and hence, return on total assets should be measured using returns accruing to both sets of stakeholders. Therefore, EBIT is the correct measure of profits to compute ROA. Whether EBIT should be taken pre-tax or post-tax could be a matter of convenience or purpose. NOPAT is nothing but post-tax EBIT and it measures the actual efficiency of a firm's investment and operating decisions that matters to the contributors of capital, after paying off statutory dues.

We have modified the traditional DuPont equation into an alternative formulation that clearly delineates the financial decision impact from the operational and investment decisions impact. The middle term, that is, ROA, captures the performance of the business and is not affected by how the firm is financed, specifically the financial leverage employed. The remaining two terms capture the extent of leverage employed and its impact on ROE.

For a firm that is completely financed with equity, both the first and third terms have a value of one and resultantly, ROE is equal to ROA. It is very interesting to observe the range of values that RES and LEV can take as the firm starts employing financial leverage, or taking debt. As leverage increases, LEV increases and RES reduces due to the interest burden on the firm. So the first condition for our formulation is that this does not apply to interest-free debt. Interest-free debt unilaterally improves ROE, without any burden on profits. Of course, an inordinate amount of even interest-free debt can cause financial distress as principal still needs to be repaid.

So theoretically, LEV takes values from 1 to infinity while RES takes values from 1 to negative infinity as leverage increases. Consequently, optimization of debt is all about balancing the two terms. Taking debt on the balance sheet in order to improve returns for shareholders is popularly called trading on equity. So long as the product of RES and LEV is greater than unity, trading on equity is beneficial to equity holders and ROE is greater than ROA. So what is that optimum level beyond which leverage starts to reduce returns for the shareholder?

For ROE to be greater than ROA,

$$\text{RES} \times \text{LEV has to be} \geq 1$$

or,

$$[1 - (\text{Int/EBIT})] \times (\text{Assets/Equity}) \geq 1$$

or,

$$[1 - \{(k_d \times D)/\text{EBIT}\}] \times [(E + D)/E] \geq 1$$

where, k_d is interest rate on debt, D is amount of debt, and E is the amount of equity.

Upon multiplying the two terms in the first box bracket with the second term, we get

$$[(E + D)/E] - [(k_d \times D) \times (Assets)/(EBIT \times E)] \geq 1$$

or,

$$1 + (D/E) - [\{k_d \times (D/E) \times (1 - t)\}/ROA]^8 \geq 1$$

Subtracting 1 from both sides, we are left with

$$[D/E] - [\{(D/E) \times k_d \times (1 - t)\}/ROA] \geq 0$$

This simplifies to

$$(D/E) \times [1 - \{k_d (1 - t)/ROA\}] \geq 0$$

And finally to

$$\boxed{ROA \geq k_d (1 - t)} \qquad (6)$$

This is a very important result. For financial leverage to improve returns for equity holders, the firm should earn returns on assets greater than its posttax cost of debt. What about a firm that pays no income tax for whatever reason? It will have to earn ROA greater than its pretax cost of debt, which is a higher threshold. Taxes on interest provide a shield and reduce their effective cost of borrowing. This allows firms to earn a lower return on their assets and still improve ROE.

When a firm that is making profits on its operations decides to introduce debt into its capital structure, the product of RES and LEV is typically greater than 1. LEV increases by much more than RES reduces. This immediately leads to an enhancing effect on ROE and benefits the shareholders as shown by the upward movement in ROE/ROA ratio in Figure 2.3. As greater leverage is introduced, there reaches a point (point C

---

[8] Assets/EBIT in the second term is written as 1/ROA.

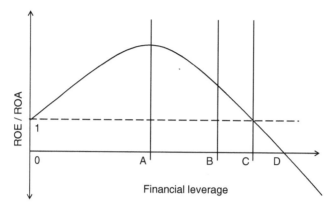

Figure 2.3 Impact of increasing financial leverage on ROE

in Figure 2.3) when RES reduces by much more than LEV increases and their product is less than 1. Now, ROE is less than ROA. In other words, the condition imposed by expression (5) is violated and ROA is now less than the posttax cost of debt. How does this happen? What has changed? Assuming operations undergo no change, as a firm piles on leverage, lenders become circumspect and more cautious. The credit risk of the firm increases and the cost at which funds are now lent to the firm, that is, k_d, increases. So even while ROA remains constant, k_d reaches a point where the posttax cost of debt exceeds ROA. Remember, the pretax cost of debt, that is, k_d, has surpassed ROA at a lower level of leverage already at point B!

Going further, ROE/ROA turns negative when leverage reaches point D. What has happened here? Is the firm necessarily losing money in its operations? Not at all. The ROA of the firm could remain intact and positive while it could be eroding shareholder wealth. When the firm reaches point D, the interest expense has surpassed EBIT making RES negative. How does this show up in the financial statements? Yes, the P&L statement will indicate positive EBIT but negative PBT and hence, negative PAT. Thus, the firm's operations though healthy are unable to lift the burden of interest laden by the high financial leverage taken. Therefore, it is important that management is well aware of how much heavy lifting the operations of their firm are capable of before taking on high leverage.

The reader should note that throughout the trajectory depicted in Figure 2.3, ROA is in the positive zone. If EBIT turns negative thereby turning ROA (and hence, ROE) negative, the ROE/ROA ratio will become positive! This is a meaningless ratio that cannot be interpreted or compared. Hence, these indicators have to be used with caution and more importantly, with understanding of the context. Hence, reiterating the importance of deciphering the story underlying the numbers.

Looking at Figure 2.3, it is clear that ideally the firm should stop loading debt at point A when the ROE/ROA ratio is at its maximum. The region A to B also affords the shareholders the benefit of financial leverage as ROE is still greater than ROA. However, the optimal point has been breached at point A. A firm in need of funding that will help enhance productivity of operations and profitability in due course may chart the path of A to B. However, the moment the firm reaches point B where ROA equals k_d, it should stop although ROA is still greater than k_d $(1 - t)$. The region from B to C is dangerous territory where the firm is still showing higher ROE but this is only because of the tax break the interest expense receives. This is not because of the firm's operational efficiency versus cost of borrowing. If for any reason the effective tax rate decreases or the firm's operations slide, the shareholders will start losing value; they will be funding to service the firm's debt. To provide a perspective, during the year 2016 to 2017, 80 nonfinancial firms from the common sample of three stock market indices of the Mumbai Stock Exchange of India namely, the BSE 500, BSE MidCap, and BSE SmallCap, were reported[9] to be unable to service interest on debt due to inadequate operating profit. This was attributed to the disruption caused by the one-time event of currency demonetization undertaken by the Indian government in November 2016 as well as the continued slowdown in the industrial and construction sectors during the year. Firms that have high financial leverage have lesser margin to deal with unanticipated events or economic slowdown that can affect operating profits.

This framework helps get a good grip on the optimality of a firm's financial leverage and its vulnerability to financial distress. In subsequent chapters we will apply this framework to different types of businesses. The reader will notice that this framework becomes more relevant for firms

---

[9]Kant, K. 2017. "14% Rise in Corporate Debt Under Stress," *Business Standard*, December 6, 2017, p. 4.

in industries that are highly levered or firms that have significant debt in their capital structure. Second, as already mentioned earlier, this framework works when the firm is making operating profits, that is, EBIT is greater than zero. A positive EBIT implies a positive ROA (ATR can never be less than zero). What happens when a firm is making operating losses? Does this framework hold in such cases?

Clearly, when EBIT is negative, RES becomes positive and larger as financial leverage increases! Therefore, the product of RES and LEV goes on increasing as financial leverage increases. What is the implication of an increasing RES $\times$ LEV multiple in such situations? The product of RES and LEV is the combined enhancing effect of financial leverage on ROA. So when ROA is positive, a high RES $\times$ LEV helps enhance the effect of a positive ROA for the firm's shareholders. Similarly, when the firm is making operating losses, a high RES $\times$ LEV amplifies the losses for the shareholders and increases their burden manifold! Hence, financial leverage is a double-edged sword that needs to be very carefully wielded.

Having examined the impact of financial leverage, we can return our attention to the middle term, ROA. As seen earlier, the ROA is the product of the firm's operating profitability and asset utilization and is a comprehensive measure of its operational prowess. A drop in ROA or a poorer-than-peers ROA can be analyzed by breaking it up into the two component ratios to examine the source of the problem. Low profitability can be further broken up into revenue issues and cost issues. Low asset turnover can be examined by isolating the asset(s) that are being held in excess or not contributing sufficiently to revenue generation. We will discuss these in detail in subsequent chapters with specific company financials.

Tying in with the Cash Flow Statement

Most commonly used financial ratios include items from the balance sheet and the income statement. The CFS gets neglected when analysis is completely based on such ratios. The CFS holds a wealth of information and gleaning inferences and insights from it can be very useful.

The most important strength the CFS has over the other two is that it is least vulnerable to manipulation and window-dressing. It is a simple statement that begins with the opening balance of cash for the period, inflows and outflows of cash during the period, and ends with the closing balance of cash. No choice of accounting methods can affect the CFS except to the extent choice of accounting methods impact tax liability. This is a very important feature of the CFS that needs to be leveraged as the business world moves toward new business models where accounting treatments are evolving and as it moves toward IFRS, which is more principle-based and gives greater autonomy to firms with respect to accounting treatments. All cash flows are categorized into three buckets corresponding to the three primary activities of a business as laid out in Figure 1.4 earlier. What should the net cash flows in each bucket look like? Positive, negative, or does it not matter?

Let us take the example of a single-business firm, say, a restaurant. When it sets out, it needs investments to establish and operate. This necessarily comes from external sources, whether debt or equity. This is a situation where CFO = 0 or negative, CFI is negative, and CFF is positive. This implies that external funding is being used to finance both investments (meant for future growth) and operations. The restaurant will start operations, will have some revenues but may be still making losses. The above balance will persist until such time the restaurant scales up and starts making cash profits. Now, CFO is positive, CFI will continue to be negative if the owner is planning improvements and expansion and CFF might continue to be positive to the extent CFO falls short of CFI needs. When the business matures, that is, further growth is marginal or nil and operations are steady, CFO is large enough to not only sustain current operations and marginal investments required for maintenance and normal growth, but to also service finance taken from external sources. This trajectory is captured in Figure 2.4.

The figure illustrates the trajectory described earlier. The number of years a firm might spend at each stage will vary across industry, economy, and time period. Firms typically begin looking at new product or business lines when they realize that their flagship product (P1) has reached maturity and does not have any further growth potential. This was popularized by the BCG matrix© as a *cash cow©*. Before the cash cow fades into oblivion, the firm would like to have another

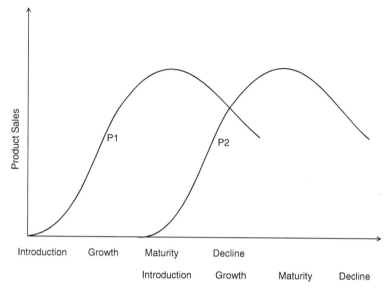

Figure 2.4 Cash flows over life-cycle stages of a firm

star©[10] (P2) in the making that would carry the firm over the next few years/decades. At this point, investment needs in P2 climb and CFO from P1 become a significant contributor to CFI requirements for P2. Net CFI may remain positive or go negative depending on the balance between CFO from P1 versus CFI needs of P2. Figure 2.4 depicts only two product life cycles for illustration purposes. In further chapters, this schema will be applied to companies to understand and evaluate their performance and strategies.

Tying in the ratio analysis with cash flows becomes critical when companies use accounting policies that can show profits or smooth earnings. In such situations, the pattern of cash flows from operations provides a clearer picture of the actual scenario.

Synthesis and Storytelling

This is the point we tie in everything to build a logical story. What is the current state of affairs at the firm with respect to profitability, solvency,

---

[10]Cash cow and Star are two of the four ways in which businesses are categorized in the BCG matrix developed by the consulting firm of the same name. The other two are Question Marks and Dogs.

liquidity, and overall performance? What decisions of the management have led the firm to the current situation, whether good or bad? What has the business strategy of the firm been? Does the strategy seem to have worked? Has the firm been equally responsible to all stakeholders? Have they ensured the interest of some stakeholders at the cost of others? At this point it is important to understand that while financial statements can provide a window to the firm's relationship with multiple stakeholders, it has its limitations.

Certain stakeholders have a direct financial relationship with the firm such as shareholders, lenders, suppliers, customers, employees, etc. and it is possible to deduce partially or substantially the value that the firm is creating for them and the relationship the firm maintains with them. However, certain other stakeholders including the society, the community, the environment, etc. have an indirect relationship with the firm and the firm's interaction with them need not reflect directly in its financial statements. One has to go beyond the numbers into qualitative information provided in the firm's annual reports, website, investor calls, and meetings in order to get an understanding of the extent to which the firm is executing its responsibility toward social and sustainability causes.

Having said this, financial statements have to be read together with qualitative information including the notes to accounts, risk factors, and management's discussion and analysis in order to draw up a nearly complete story.

CHAPTER 3

Analyzing a Products-Based Firm's Financial Statements

In this chapter we pick up firms that deal in tangible goods, either as manufacturer-sellers or as traders. They could be business-to-business (B2B) or business-to-customer (B2C) firms. Before we begin, we need to understand what is unique or different about these firms as compared to firms dealing in services. In fact, this is the first step in any financial analysis—to understand the business of the firm from their financial statements and other information available.

Differences in Financials of Goods- and Services-Based Firms

Take a look at the common-size statements of two firms in Tables 3.1 to 3.3. Can you identify the firm dealing in goods and the one dealing in services? What are the distinguishing features?

Table 3.1 Split of components of income statements across industries

Components of the Income Statement	Company A	Company B
Material cost as % of sales	26%	Nil
Employee cost as % of sales	10.3%	49.5%
Gross profit margin	64%	51.5%
Operating costs as % of Sales (including material cost)	80%	69%
Depreciation as % of sales	4.6%	2%
Operating profit (EBIT) margin	22%	31%
Interest expenses as % of sales	3.5%	Nil
Net profit margin	11.6%	28%

Table 3.2 Split of components of balance sheets across industries

Components of the Balance Sheet	Company A	Company B
Fixed assets as % of total assets	42%	13%
Inventory as % of current assets	49%	Nil
Cash as % of current assets	7%	63%
Current assets as % of total assets	12%	63%
Long-term debt as % of total liabilities	19%	Nil
Short-term debt as % of current liabilities	25%	Nil
Trade payables as % of current liabilities	37%	4%
Current liabilities as % of total liabilities	17%	21%

Table 3.3 Split of components of cash flows across industries

Components of the Cash Flow Statement	Company A	Company B
Capex as % of profit after tax	118%	15%
Working capital as % of cash from operations	21%	18%
Dividends as % of profit after tax	24%	43%
Proceeds from borrowings as % of CFF	More than 5×	Nil
Repayment of borrowings as % of CFF	More than 4×	Nil

Note: Capex stands for capital expenditures; CFF stands for cash flows from financing activities.

You guessed right! Company A deals in goods, while Company B deals in services. These firms are Tata Steel Ltd., one of India's largest and oldest steel manufacturers, and Infosys Ltd., the information technology major, respectively[1]. What are the giveaways? First, B holds no inventory and has no material-related costs. A firm producing or trading in goods has to maintain some inventory. Second, employee costs take away 50 percent of revenues for B; it is clearly a service firm whose major resource is human capital. Company A holds substantial fixed assets and inventory; high inventory indicates that A deals in goods and high fixed assets indicates that it is probably a manufacturing firm and not a trading firm. A's capital expenditure is also very high in relation to its PAT, further strengthening this hypothesis. This is not to say that trading firms or even service firms may not have large holdings

---

[1]Financials for Tata Steel Ltd. and Infosys Ltd. have been sourced from their respective annual reports for the financial year 2016–17.

of fixed assets. If they do, the category of fixed assets will be very different—manufacturing firms will be heavily invested in plant and machinery, while trading and service firms may have higher holdings of land and buildings in the form of warehouses or office spaces, respectively. Infosys Ltd. holds vast amounts of real estate as it has built huge campuses across cities in India.

Another striking difference between the two firms is the amount of debt held and hence, interest liability of Company A versus Company B. A is clearly using debt in its capital structure, which might indicate need for heavy investment, long gestation periods for capex, and the presence of high value of tangible assets that can be put up as collateral for loans. Does it mean that service firms always run an unleveraged balance sheet? Not necessarily. But they are typically more cautious with debt and prefer more equity than debt funding. Why is this so?

The primary reason is that service businesses more often do not require large amounts of capital for setting up and for continuing operations. They can normally be set up with much lesser capital and achieve breakeven faster. Second, service companies do not own as much tangible assets as manufacturing/trading firms to provide collateral for large-scale debt. This is also a reason service businesses hold more cash and cash equivalents than goods-based businesses. In the absence of fixed assets that can be used during downturns or difficult times to either raise debt funding or that can be sold to raise funds, service firms have to hold cash-based assets to see them through difficult times.

This first-level understanding of the major differences between goods-based and service-based businesses and the reasons for these differences helps us put their financial ratios into perspective and analyze them more meaningfully.

Applying the DuPont Analysis to a Goods-Based Business

Provided in Tables 3.4 and 3.5 are the P&L statements and balance sheets, respectively, of Hindustan Unilever Ltd., the Indian subsidiary of Unilever, Plc. (HUL), for 5 years[2].

---

[2]Financial statements of Hindustan Unilever Ltd. have been sourced from the Ace Analyzer database.

Table 3.4 Profit and loss statements for HUL

	For year ended 31st day of				
	March 2017	March 2016	March 2015	March 2014	March 2013
Gross sales	358.49	347.33	339.03	307.97	284.87
Less: Excise	25.97	24.30	19.31	15.63	14.83
Net sales	332.52	323.03	319.72	292.34	270.04
Expenditure					
Raw materials consumed	137.50	132.67	135.66	124.73	119.22
Power and fuel cost	2.95	3.09	3.47	3.63	3.36
Employee cost	17.43	16.80	17.24	15.73	14.13
Other mfg. expenses	39.56	38.70	39.16	34.83	31.09
Gen. and admin. expenses	5.66	5.67	5.88	5.49	5.42
Sales and dist. expenses	50.58	51.78	54.04	50.29	44.89
Miscellaneous expenses	15.57	14.19	10.18	10.39	9.90
Total expenditure	**269.25**	**262.90**	**265.63**	**245.10**	**227.99**
EBITDA	63.27	60.13	54.10	47.24	42.05
Depreciation	4.32	3.53	3.22	2.95	2.51
EBIT	58.95	56.60	50.88	44.30	39.54
Other income	3.69	4.24	5.70	5.91	5.32
Interest	0.35	0.17	0.18	0.41	0.26
Exceptional net income	2.37	(0.31)	6.79	2.36	6.06
Profit before tax	64.66	60.36	63.20	52.15	50.66
Provision for tax	19.76	18.76	19.44	12.59	12.27
PAT	**44.90**	**41.60**	**43.76**	**39.56**	**38.39**

Note: All amounts are in INR (Indian rupees) billion.

Unless the analysis is for a specific purpose or from a specific point of view, for example, lending decision, assessing working capital management, etc., the first step in any financial analysis is to figure out the aspects of the firm that require a deep-dive. Drawing up common-size versions of

Table 3.5 Balance sheets for HUL

	As on 31st				
	March 2017	March 2016	March 2015	March 2014	March 2013
Sources of funds					
Share capital	2.16	2.16	2.16	2.16	2.16
Reserves	65.50	63.77	38.36	33.43	26.69
Shareholder funds	67.66	65.93	40.52	35.60	28.86
Total debts	12.26	11.33	11.76	12.78	12.01
Total liabilities	**79.92**	**77.26**	**52.28**	**48.37**	**40.86**
Fixed assets	72.96	57.97	54.12	50.79	44.18
Less: Accumulated depn.	28.56	25.17	25.91	23.33	19.86
Net block	44.40	32.80	28.21	27.46	24.31
Capital work in progress	2.29	4.08	5.16	3.73	2.22
Investments	44.84	31.75	36.13	33.85	29.71
Total noncurrent assets	91.53	68.63	69.50	65.04	56.25
Inventories	25.41	27.26	28.49	29.40	27.06
Sundry debtors	10.85	12.64	10.10	10.17	9.97
Cash and bank	18.28	30.09	26.89	25.16	19.01
Other current assets	3.48	3.08	3.00	2.75	2.11
Loans and advances	5.81	4.56	4.32	3.22	4.45
Total current assets	63.83	77.63	72.80	70.70	62.59
Less: Current Liabilities & Provisions					
Current liabilities	73.22	67.74	64.94	68.29	60.17
Provisions	3.92	2.93	27.08	20.88	19.88
Total current liabilities	77.14	70.67	92.02	89.17	80.06
Net current assets	(13.31)	6.96	(19.22)	(18.46)	(17.47)
Deferred tax assets/liab.	1.70	1.67	1.99	1.80	2.09
Total assets	**79.92**	**77.26**	**52.28**	**48.37**	**40.86**
Contingent liabilities	10.58	10.46	9.91	9.91	8.20

Note: All amounts in INR billion.

the financial statements is a good place to begin. It simply means expressing all items in the P&L statement as percentage of sales or total revenues (Table 3.6) and all items in the balance sheet as percentage of total balance sheet size (Table 3.7). Let's see what HUL's numbers look like.

Table 3.6 Common-size version of HUL's P&L statement (all items as % of gross sales)

| | For year ended 31st day of | | | | |
	March 2017	March 2016	March 2015	March 2014	March 2013
Gross sales	100	100	100	100	100
Less: Excise	7	7	6	5	5
Net sales	93	93	94	95	95
Expenditure					
Materials cost	38	38	40	41	42
Power and fuel cost	1	1	1	1	1
Employee cost	5	5	5	5	5
Other mfg. expenses	11	11	12	11	11
G&A expenses	2	2	2	2	2
S&D expenses	14	15	16	16	16
Misc. expenses	4	4	3	3	3
Total expenses	75	76	78	80	80
EBITDA	18	17	16	15	15
Depreciation	1	1	1	1	1
EBIT	16	16	15	14	14
Other income	1.0	1.2	1.7	1.9	1.8
Interest	0.1	0.0	0.1	0.1	0.1
Exceptional items	1	0	2	1	2
PBT	18	17	18	17	17
Provision for tax	5	5	6	4	4
PAT	12	12	13	13	13

Table 3.7 Common-size version of balance sheets for HUL (all items as % of total assets or total liabilities)

| | As on 31st | | | | |
	March 2017	March 2016	March 2015	March 2014	March 2013
Share capital	3	3	5	6	7
Reserves	97	97	95	94	93
Shareholder funds	85	85	78	74	71
Total debts	15	15	22	26	29
Total liabilities	100	100	100	100	100

Table 3.7 (continued)

	As on 31st				
	March 2017	March 2016	March 2015	March 2014	March 2013
Fixed assets	91	75	104	105	108
Less: Acc. depn. as % of fixed assets	39	43	48	46	45
Net block	56	42	54	57	60
Capital WIP	3	5	10	8	5
Investments	56	41	69	70	73
Total noncurrent assets	115	89	133	134	138
Current assets as % of total current assets					
Inventories	40	35	39	42	43
Sundry debtors	17	16	14	14	16
Cash and bank	29	39	37	36	30
Other current assets	5	4	4	4	3
Loans and advances	9	6	6	5	7
Total current assets	80	100	139	146	153
Current liabilities as % of total current liabilities					
Current liabilities	95	96	71	77	75
Provisions	5	4	29	23	25
Total current liabilities	97	91	176	184	196
Net current assets	(17)	9	(37)	(38)	(43)
Deferred tax assets/ liabilities	2	2	4	4	5
Total assets	100	100	100	100	100
Contingent liabilities	13	14	19	20	20

The common-size statements reveal trends and areas that require attention over others. Some of the aspects of HUL that stand out from the above two statements are as follows:

1. No item in the P&L statement has changed by more than 4 percentage points over the 5-year period. The maximum change is seen in material costs that have reduced from 42 percent of gross sales in FY2013 to 38 percent in FY2017. For a manufacturing business, this is a significant achievement and a boost to the bottom-line.

This is evident from the 3 and 2 percentage points improvements in EBITDA and EBIT margins, respectively, over the period.

2. Despite improvements in operating and pretax profit margins, the net profit margin has reduced by a percentage point over the period. This is clearly on account of the provisions for taxes. This could be an area of interest for an analyst or potential equity investor.

3. Interest expenses account for a miniscule portion of gross sales. Prima facie, it indicates that interest burden and consequently, financial leverage may not be an area that warrants much investigation. But it will do well to confirm this hypothesis by computing interest expenses as a percentage of EBIT and to take a look at the financial leverage the firm is carrying. For all the years, interest expenses as a percentage of EBIT (which has been in a healthy 14 percent to 16 percent range) is less than 1 percent, indicating that the company is very comfortable in meeting its interest obligations. However, their financial leverage is 15 percent in FY2017 and it was close to 30 percent in FY2013. This is not very low leverage and there seems an apparent dichotomy between the financial leverage and interest burden. A quick, back-of-the-envelope calculation for average interest rate for HUL reveals a very low average rate of 3 percent for FY2017 and FY2013 showing an unbelievable 0.1 percent! This should pique the curiosity of the analyst to investigate the sources and terms of borrowings HUL has obtained. Average cost of borrowing in India for the best rated firms cannot be less than 7 percent to 10 percent per annum.

4. Other income is also a very low proportion of total revenues, which is a sign of comfort.

5. Turning our attention to Table 3.7, we see that reserves and surpluses have been steadily contributing more to shareholder funds, which indicates healthy business.

6. Fixed assets constitute more than 90 percent of total assets and were over 100 percent of total assets in FY2013! How is this possible? We quickly discover that this is because of the format in which the balance sheet has been presented. There are two ways to present the

balance sheet, where total assets equal total liabilities. The format introduced in Figure 1.2 previously was

Noncurrent assets + Current assets = Shareholder equity
                                  + Noncurrent liabilities
                                  + Current liabilities

This can be re-presented as

Noncurrent assets + (Current assets − Current liabilities)
    = Shareholder funds + Noncurrent liabilities

The term in brackets is net current assets, also referred to as net working capital. Current assets are assets that arise in the ordinary course of a firm's operations and get used up and replaced in short periods of time—over the firm's operating cycle. Current liabilities also arise as part of operational transactions and provide outside funding for part of the current asset requirement. The portion of current assets not funded by current liabilities has to be funded using longer term sources of finance such as shareholder equity and/ or long-term debt.

The reader can now understand that noncurrent assets for HUL are more than 100 percent of total assets because its net working capital is negative for all the years except one where it was a small positive. This warrants an analyst's attention and investigation.

7. Let us first complete our discussion on fixed assets. At over 90 percent of total assets, clearly the firm is heavily invested into fixed assets and this is not surprising as HUL has manufacturing operations. However, the gap between gross and net fixed assets is interesting. It shows that fixed assets existing on March 31, 2017, were depreciated to the extent of almost 40 percent. This might indicate that the firm is using old assets or could be the effect of its depreciation policies. Applying 25 percent depreciation on reducing balance each year will bring the value of the asset to 40 percent in less than 4 years. An increasing trend in the net fixed assets percentage does indicate that the firm is investing in new assets.

8. Let's now return to HUL's negative net current assets. Is this a deliberate strategy? What does it mean for liquidity? What does it indicate about the company's position in its market? Keeping in view the financially sound and profitable position of the company, it seems that maintaining a negative net working capital or having a current ratio of less than 1, is a deliberate strategy. This means that not only are the current liabilities or outsiders such as vendors, employees, or service providers funding all of HUL's current assets, but they are also financing part of the company's long-term assets. The company does not have to use its shareholder funds or long-term debts to fund working capital and some more! This is a big bonus from a financing viewpoint.

Clearly, HUL wields immense bargaining power with both its customers and suppliers to get such favorable terms as is evident from its receivables outstanding (less than 13 days of sales) as against payables outstanding of between 175 and 200 days of purchases[3] across the last 4 years. Does this enviable position come without risks? Not at all! This position has been earned by HUL over years of being in the Indian FMCG market and is an enviable one so long as the going is good. Any hint of trouble or financial distress either within the company or from the external environment can cause at least temporary liquidity pressures[4] if creditors come calling all together for their monies.

So what is the assessment of the company after this first-level analysis? Their financial health seems stable with none of the parameters showing much volatility over the last 5 years. Financial leverage and interest burden is not a problem for the firm. Its market standing is solid as evidenced by its net working capital (how do we know this is not due to

---

[3]With bulk of the current liabilities being trade payables we have taken the entire balance of current liabilities, excluding provisions to compute this figure. The idea is to get a sense of the market dynamics rather than accuracy, given the wide margin between receivables and payable days outstanding.

[4]A good example of this is the "demonetization" of rupees 500 and 1000 currencies that was declared overnight by the Government of India on 8th November, 2016. Panic and cash crunch that ensued saw many small businesses and traders lose business and many shutting shop. The effect of the move had ripple effects in the economy and continued for almost a year across supply chains.

Table 3.8 DuPont analysis for HUL

	For year ended 31st day of			
	March 2017	March 2016	March 2015	March 2014
ROE (LHS)	67.22%	78.16%	114.97%	122.75%
Interest burden (1 − RES)	0.89%	0.45%	0.56%	1.28%
NOPAT margin	10.93%	10.89%	9.27%	10.29%
ATR	8.90	5.36	6.74	6.90
LEV	0.60	1.22	1.32	1.38
ROE (RHS)	58.15%	70.77%	82.14%	97.11%
ROE difference (LHS vs. RHS)	9.07%	7.38%	32.83%	25.64%
ROA from operations	97.26%	58.42%	62.47%	71.05%

illiquidity?) and low average rate of interest at which the firm has sourced debt funds. We can now conduct the DuPont analysis which will either confirm our hypothesis that all is well with the company or that its operational performance needs working upon.

The 4-way DuPont formulation states ROE = RES × NOPAT margin × ATR × LEV.

Let us plug in the direct computation of ROE, that is, NPM divided by Average shareholder equity on the LHS and the component values on the RHS for the recent 4 years.[5]

At first glance, what stands out most starkly in the case of HUL's DuPont analysis? First, that the ROE computation in the LHS does not equal the RHS; the latter indicates lower ROE. Second, that ROE is far lower than ROA from operations for FY2017. Let us handle the second issue first. We learned earlier that ROA translates into higher ROE for equity holders when leverage is brought into the capital structure, while the interest burden is contained well within healthy operating profits, thereby taking the product of RES and LEV to greater than unity. For a company such as HUL, leverage has been moderate and interest burden negligible. Then why is ROE less than ROA? Is this indeed dilution of returns for equity holders?

At this point the following question becomes relevant: In our derivation of the DuPont framework we had understood that the lower bound

---

[5]Since we use average values of assets and shareholder equity, we can work out the DuPont parameters only for 4 years.

Table 3.9 DuPont analysis for HUL on gross assets basis

	For year ended 31st day of			
	March 2017	March 2016	March 2015	March 2014
ROE (direct computation)	67.22%	78.16%	114.97%	122.75%
Interest burden	0.89%	0.45%	0.56%	1.28%
NOPAT margin	10.93%	10.89%	9.27%	10.29%
ATR	3.19	3.15	3.26	3.22
LEV	1.68	2.07	2.73	2.96
ROE (indirect computation)	58.15%	70.77%	82.14%	97.11%
Difference in ROE (direct vs. indirect)	9.07%	7.38%	32.83%	25.64%
ROA from operations	34.83%	34.29%	30.22%	33.19%

of LEV is unity. How is LEV for FY2017 working to less than unity? A closer look at the balance sheet of HUL will reveal that its net worth is greater than total assets! How is this possible?

The answer lies in its negative net working capital. But more on this later. Let us first recast the balance sheet by listing all assets under the uses of funds and all liabilities under sources. This will require removing the current liabilities as a deduction from current assets on the asset side of the balance sheet and instead listing them among the sources of funds or the liabilities side, taking total (gross) operating assets[6] (and total liabilities) as on March 31, 2017, to INR 110.52 billion. Shareholder equity is now lesser than total assets, giving us an LEV of greater than unity. Let us rework our DuPont table using gross assets and see whether our inferences about HUL's performance change.

What metrics have changed now? Naturally, only the ones involving total assets as a variable will change, that is, ATR and LEV. We notice that ATR has reduced significantly as revenues are now spread over a larger asset base. LEV too, increases as the numerator is now gross assets—a larger measure. Understandably, this reworking has no impact on ROE as both profits and equity base remain unchanged. Significant, however, is the change in ROA. ROA is the product of NOPAT, which remains unchanged, and ATR, which has significantly reduced. Hence, the revised ROA is significantly lower than in Table 3.8. The same operating profit is

---

[6]Excluding investments

now spread over a larger asset base, thereby giving us a lower measure of ROA. Comparing this ROA to ROE helps us see how healthy financial leverage employed by HUL has helped it to provide its equity holders returns of over 20 percentage points over ROA for FY2017 (and even more so in the previous years).

Does this mean that the ROA of 34.83 percent is a correct measure and that 97.26 percent is incorrect? Not necessarily. The measure of 97.26 percent is based on a calculation that only takes into account assets to the extent they are financed using long term sources of finance, i.e. equity and long-term debt. Long-term fundingis meant to be used to fund long-term assets and a portion of the working capital, considered the permanent portion of the working capital. The fluctuating portion of the working capital is meant to be funded by current liabilities. In the case of HUL, however, the current liabilities are funding not only the fluctuating portion of the current assets but also the permanent portion as well as some portion of the long-term assets! This is indicated by its negative net working capital. As a result of this, long-term assets financed by long-term sources of funds are very low, thereby inflating ROA. This measure of ROA coincides with return on capital invested (ROIC), where capital invested comprises long-term sources of funding only. Here, the perspective changes from understanding returns generated by utilization of assets to returns generated on long-term funds deployed; from a business efficiency view to a return to providers of capital view.

Seen from the former perspective, that is, understanding operational efficiency, there is a case for preferring the gross assets based computation (leading to ROA of 34.83 percent) as compared to the net assets based computation. ATR is calculated as revenues divided by total assets. Revenues are earned using the services of both long-term and *gross* current assets. Hence, the productivity of assets should be assessed taking into account all assets deployed in production, irrespective of their term structure or source of finance. Based on these arguments, we have analyzed firms in the rest of this book using the gross assets method.

Let us now address the first observation we had on the DuPont analysis of the RHS and LHS calculation of ROE being unequal. This is on account of the Other Income and Exceptional items components that have not been modeled in our 4-way DuPont framework. Is the difference significant? The differentials for the years ending March 31, 2014, through March 31, 2017 are 25.64 percent, 32.83 percent, 7.38 percent, and 9.07 percent, respectively. These numbers are not insignificant, especially for the earlier 2 years. The contribution of these two components has definitely come down in the latest 2 years. Is this a good sign or bad? How does one understand these figures?

High dependence on other income is not a good sign and not taken positively by investors. They invest their money in the firm's equity (or debt) in order to benefit from the firm's expertise in its core business. Therefore, ROE to the tune of 25 percent and 30 percent from noncore business is not a comfortable indication, if it persists and if it appears that a firm is depending on such income to boost its profits or overall returns. However, this is not so in the case of HUL as the ROE from its core business (the RHS computation) indicates impressive financial stability and strength. Interest burden is negligible, financial leverage is close to unity, and hence, not a large contributor to ROE.

Having addressed the apparent "discrepancies," we now turn our attention to what the analysis implies for the performance of HUL. The ROA computed as the product of the NOPAT margin and ATR stands at more than 34 percent for FY2017. Even at its lowest over the 5-year period HUL posted ROE of 58 percent in FY2017, which is very impressive. This implies that investment of a dollar (or rupee) in its assets yields the firm 34 cents (or paise), which it further converts into 58 cents for its equity holders. The next step is to figure how the firm is earning such superlative returns. Clearly, ATR is the driver here with NOPAT margin at a modest 9 percent to 11 percent across the last 4 years. This is not a surprise as FMCG businesses work on low margins; production and marketing costs taking away a chunk of their revenues. Therefore, it becomes imperative for firms in this industry to leverage their assets to the maximum and make volumes their driver for returns.

Let us turn back to our figures in Table 3.9. The RHS is modeled such as to analyze the core business of the firm. This means that the ATR should include only core revenues and core assets. Similarly, LEV should be computed only for the core assets.[7] What are core assets? Most firms' "Other Income"

---

[7]In valuation literature cash and cash equivalents are also removed to arrive at core assets. But we will retain it since firms maintain a certain amount of cash equivalents for working capital requirement. By including cash and its equivalents as part of core assets, any excess cash held will have a reducing effect on core ROA thereby, implying overinvestment in core assets.

Table 3.10 DuPont analysis for nonoperating activities of HUL

	For year ended 31st day of			
	March 2017	March 2016	March 2015	March 2014
ROA from OI	9.64%	12.49%	16.29%	18.58%
LEV	0.57	0.64	0.92	0.99
ROE from OI[8]	5.52%	7.97%	14.98%	18.33%

comprises income from investments, that is, interest and/or dividend income. The assets underlying these incomes are financial investments made by the firm. The computation for ATR in the table, therefore, accounts for all assets but for financial investments shown in the balance sheet. Also, the revenues used for ATR and NOPAT margin do not include "Other Income."

What is HUL's ROE from other income? Assuming no incremental costs are involved in earning these incomes, the profit margin in this "business line" is 100 percent. The ATR for other income is nothing but Other Income divided by Average Investments or in other words, average return on its financial investments. Assuming that both core and noncore assets enjoy the same amount of leverage, we compute the ROE from Other Income (OI) as:

$$\text{ROE}_{(OI)} = \text{OI/Average Investments} \\ \times \text{Average Investments/Average Equity}$$

Table 3.10 shows the analysis of returns from investments in financial assets for HUL.

As is evident, ROE from OI has declined both on account of ROA and LEV reducing over the years. ROA is directly a function of investment opportunities in the market and prevailing interest rates. India has seen a reducing interest rate regime over the last 4 years with inflation having been reined in very strongly.

The next step is to complete the loop by triangulating the analysis so far with information from the firm's cash flow statements provided in Table 3.11.

---

[8]The gap still persisting between ROI from other income and the difference between RHS and LHS calculation of ROE earlier is on account of exceptional items in the P&L statement.

Table 3.11 Cash flow statements for HUL

	For year ended 31st day of				
	March 2017	March 2016	March 2015	March 2014	March 2013
Profit before tax	62.29	60.58	56.40	49.80	44.60
Adjustments	1.21	(0.33)	(1.30)	(1.78)	(1.95)
Trade and other receivables	1.73	(2.57)	0.03	(0.17)	(1.49)
Inventories	1.86	0.89	0.91	(2.01)	(0.39)
Loans and advances	(1.56)	(0.04)	(1.75)	0.58	(1.40)
Trade and other payables	4.96	0.40	(2.03)	9.09	5.72
Other current assets and liab.	0.16	0.51	(0.58)	(3.43)	1.85
Changes in working capital	7.15	(0.81)	(3.42)	4.05	4.29
Tax paid	(18.59)	(17.65)	(18.62)	(13.84)	(10.74)
Extra and other items	(0.21)	(0.08)	(0.14)	(0.05)	(0.17)
Cash from operating activities	51.85	41.71	32.92	38.18	36.05
Purchase of fixed assets	(14.61)	(8.10)	(6.06)	(6.06)	(4.41)
Sale of fixed assets	0.09	0.38	0.33	0.22	0.01
Purchase of investments	(328.77)	(233.53)	(194.10)	(96.39)	(161.80)
Sale of investments	327.35	233.35	195.18	91.83	163.82
Dividend income	0.14	0.33	0.24	0.16	0.38
Interest income	2.64	3.15	2.18	2.32	2.14
Other investment activities	1.43	1.60	3.60	3.16	0.50
Cash from investing activities	(11.73)	(2.82)	1.38	(4.76)	0.63
Short-term loans	1.00	1.77	(0.01)	(0.05)	0.24
Equity dividend paid	(35.72)	(33.54)	(29.12)	(24.81)	(35.58)
Interest paid	(0.14)	(0.02)	(0.18)	(0.29)	(0.26)
Income tax on dividend paid	(7.17)	(6.73)	(5.25)	(4.23)	(5.79)
Other financial activities	(0.11)	(0.12)	(0.06)	(0.23)	(0.10)
Cash from financing activities	(42.14)	(38.64)	(34.62)	(29.60)	(41.48)
Net cash inflow/outflow	(2.02)	0.25	(0.32)	3.82	(4.80)
Opening cash and equivalents	8.37	8.12	8.44	4.62	9.42
Closing cash and equivalents	6.35	8.37	8.12	8.44	4.62

Note: All amounts in INR billion.

Strength of operations of a firm is not just the operating profits it earns but also its ability to convert these profits into cash. HUL's cash flows from operations (CFO) have been strong and consistently rising over the years except for FY2015 where a brief dip seems to be on account of heavy tax payments. The ratio of CFO to EBITDA is a good yardstick to understand the ability of a firm to convert book profits into cash. A firm artificially pushing sales and profits by giving easy credit to customers and delaying recoveries, for instance, will be discovered in this process. For the first 2 years, their cash conversion rate has been 86 percent and 81 percent, respectively, dipping to 61 percent in FY2015 and then recovering to 69 percent and 82 percent in the most recent 2 years. A closer look at the CFS will reveal that besides the heavy tax outflow, FY2015 was the only year when its cash movement with suppliers was a negative, implying the firm repaid more to its suppliers than received fresh credit from them. The reader should recollect that trade payables are a significant source of working capital for HUL.

What patterns do we see in HUL's investment activity? The firm is regularly purchasing as well as selling fixed assets. While the former is a formidable amount each year (an astute analyst will do well to dive deeper into what these investments are), the latter is miniscule in comparison. Assuming the firm is investing in operating assets such as manufacturing and storage facilities, regional and branch networks, this indicates future growth plans are in place.

Contrast this with the purchase and sale patterns for financial investments. The two numbers are almost equal! What conclusions can one draw from these two line items? First, that the amount of investments HUL has been dealing in each year is definitely nontrivial—steadily increasing since FY2014, it is almost as much as the gross sales for the firm in FY2017. Second, the firm actively manages its investments as is evident by the almost 100 percent churn with purchases and sales being almost equal! The CFS therefore, indicates that for HUL, managing financial investments is not just a passive investment of residual cash surplus but probably a strategic activity and meant to contribute to its top-line and bottom-line.

Finally, cash from financing activity is a huge negative; almost completely attributed to equity dividends and taxes thereon. What possible inferences can be drawn from this? Definitely, that shareholders at HUL expect regular and substantial dividends each year and the firm is not letting them down. But as we look at more firms' financial statements, we will see that this is a pattern for many of them. What is important here is if the firm can actually afford this dividend. HUL has been consistently generating free cash flows (FCF) and its interest payments are negligible. FCF are defined as cash from operations less investment requirement in fixed (and operating intangible) assets. Of course, the FCF just about covers the dividend payment and in some years falls short. This need not be a cause for worry when one sees consistency in cash generation from operations.

We have thus, peeled out maybe, just the first or at best, two layers of the underlying story of HUL's business and its direction in this analysis. Anyone interested in a particular aspect of their business or studying the financial statements for specific decisions will need to conduct deeper and more focused analysis.

In the rest of the chapter we will pick up more examples and restrict our discussions to only the key aspects or problem areas that the financial statements reveal.

Analyzing the Financials of a Loss-Making Firm

Provided in the following tables are the P&L statements and balance sheets of Bhushan Steels Ltd.[9], an Indian company that was pulled into insolvency proceedings in FY2017. Could an interested party have predicted financial distress and insolvency proceedings earlier on by a diligent analysis of its financial statements?

In this example we will only focus on the aspects that eventually led the firm into insolvency proceedings and what an astute analyst should have looked for. Second, certain line items such as Reserves were not delved into deeper in the case of HUL simply because the firm was consistently profitable and adding to its reserves each year and did not require external funding. Reserves are the most important component of shareholder equity and when they start to erode while shareholder wealth gets beefed up with external equity, it is time for an analyst to sit up and take notice.

What's the good news and bad news in Bhushan's P&L statement in Table 3.12? The bad news is obvious—they have seen reducing net profits year-on-year that have converted into increasing net losses since FY2015.

---

[9]Financial statements of Bhushan Steel Ltd. have been sourced from the Ace Analyzer database.

Table 3.12 Profit and loss statements for Bhushan Steels Ltd.

	For year ended 31st day of				
	March 2017	March 2016	March 2015	March 2014	March 2013
Gross sales	150.27	131.24	117.35	106.00	118.00
Less: Excise	13.21	13.21	10.89	9.25	10.56
Net sales	137.06	118.03	106.46	96.76	107.44
Expenditure					
Material cost	65.54	62.03	59.80	51.94	58.37
Power and fuel cost	12.54	12.29	12.43	9.03	8.55
Employee cost	4.91	4.36	2.58	1.89	1.73
Other manufacturing expenses	11.53	7.57	3.91	3.46	2.82
General and admin. Expenses	4.15	3.20	0.84	0.56	0.00
Selling and distribution expenses	8.36	7.58	5.07	2.65	2.78
Miscellaneous expenses	0.81	0.39	0.11	0.34	0.09
Total expenditure	107.85	97.42	84.73	69.86	74.34
EBITDA	**29.21**	**20.61**	**21.72**	**26.90**	**33.10**
Depreciation	16.86	17.30	9.38	9.64	8.31
EBIT	**12.36**	**3.31**	**12.34**	**17.26**	**24.80**
Other income and excep. Items	0.65	0.76	0.02	0.29	0.17
Interest expenses	54.27	46.01	24.94	16.63	12.87
Profit before tax	**(41.26)**	**(41.95)**	**(12.58)**	**0.92**	**12.09**
Provision for tax	(6.24)	(8.64)	(0.01)	0.33	3.05
Profits after tax	**(35.02)**	**(33.30)**	**(12.57)**	**0.58**	**9.04**

Note: All figures are in rupees billion.

Shareholder equity has hence, started to get eroded. This clearly indicates serious issues with the business. The good news, however, is that the firm has been seeing not only increasing revenues but seems to be running profitable core operations—its operating income (EBITDA and EBIT) is still positive and seems to have revived in FY2017 after consistently dropping over the previous 4 years.

What are the giveaways in Bhushan's financial statements until FY2016 that could have hinted at the impending bankruptcy besides the dipping operating profits we saw earlier?

An operationally profitable firm is posting huge net losses that are eroding shareholder wealth simply because of its massive interest obligations as indicated in its balance sheets in Table 3.13. Clearly, financial leverage is an issue with Bhushan. Long-term debt has increased at the rate of 16 percent, 13 percent, and 2 percent during FY2014,

Table 3.13 Balance sheets for Bhushan Steels Ltd.

	For year ended 31st day of				
	March 2017	March 2016	March 2015	March 2014	March 2013
Sources of funds					
Equity—paid up	0.45	0.45	0.45	0.45	0.44
Preference capital paid up	0.00	0.00	1.30	1.04	1.02
Share capital	0.45	0.45	1.76	1.49	1.45
Securities premium	7.26	7.26	32.97	33.08	33.86
P&L balance and gen. reserve	(26.26)	9.89	37.27	50.01	50.08
Capital and specified reserves	3.72	3.70	7.06	7.03	6.86
Total reserves	(15.28)	20.85	77.31	90.13	90.80
Shareholder funds	**(14.83)**	**21.30**	**79.06**	**91.62**	**92.26**
Minority interest	(0.01)	0.08	0.33	0.33	0.76
Secured loans	304.87	321.95	308.98	255.30	210.53
Unsecured loans	1.70	1.63	6.70	22.03	27.96
Total debts	306.58	323.58	315.68	277.33	238.49
Total liabilities	**291.74**	**344.96**	**395.07**	**369.28**	**331.51**
Application of funds					
Fixed assets	551.79	531.65	416.82	261.19	214.44
Less: Accumulated depreciation	34.15	17.30	51.19	42.43	32.95
Net block	517.64	514.36	365.64	218.76	181.49
Capital work in progress	11.71	27.29	27.87	165.91	93.44
Preoperative expenses pending	0.00	0.00	0.00	0.00	35.04
Investments	14.85	16.26	19.32	21.87	29.48
Inventories	31.49	20.99	73.21	64.80	55.60
Sundry debtors	15.26	11.82	23.98	24.64	23.43

Table 3.13 (continued)

	For year ended 31st day of				
	March 2017	March 2016	March 2015	March 2014	March 2013
Cash and bank	1.56	1.64	0.88	0.85	1.64
Other current assets	3.61	2.86	8.82	3.51	0.00
Loans and advances	6.05	3.76	9.80	10.76	15.28
Total current assets	57.96	41.07	116.69	104.57	95.95
Less: Current liabilities and provisions					
Sundry creditors	11.10	11.76	27.39	23.52	16.32
Interest accrued but not due	57.56	16.02	7.90	4.85	2.25
Other liabilities	206.56	184.79	85.33	99.26	71.14
Provisions	0.05	0.04	0.08	0.43	0.77
Total current liabilities	275.27	212.61	120.71	128.07	90.47
Net current assets	(217.31)	(171.54)	(4.02)	(23.50)	5.48
Deferred tax assets/ liabilities	(35.15)	(41.40)	(13.74)	(13.75)	(13.43)
Total assets	291.74	344.96	395.07	369.28	331.50
Contingent liabilities	35.76	28.89	13.46	10.61	6.82

Note: All amounts are in INR billion.

FY2015, and FY2016, respectively. While this does not in itself seem alarming, the impact of this borrowing is visible in the long-term debt to equity ratios (D/E) for these years—2.6× in FY2013, 3.99× in FY2015, zooming up to over 15× in FY2016. The D/E ratio is a function of the increasing borrowings as well as the rapidly declining shareholder equity.

The other line item that signals possible problems is the rapid rise in Other Current Liabilities (OCL). These are significantly high both in value and growth rate. A deeper dive into this line item in Bhushan's annual reports reveals that they comprise current portion of long-term debt, repayment overdue on these debts, interest *accrued and due* on borrowings, and unpaid matured debentures and interest accrued thereon. In other words, the firm had started defaulting on its debt servicing since FY2015.

Let us now see in Table 3.14 what the DuPont Analysis of Bhushan's financials reveals.

Table 3.14 DuPont analysis for Bhushan Steels Ltd.

	For year ended 31st day of			
	March 2017	March 2016	March 2015	March 2014
ROE (direct computation)	(1,071.63)%	(66.10)%	(14.67)%	0.63%
Interest burden	291.83%	384.94%	201.93%	98.28%
NOPAT margin	12.37%	9.11%	10.52%	15.97%
ATR	0.26	0.24	0.23	0.24
LEV	179.01	10.85	5.83	4.84
ROE (indirect computation)	(1,091.52)%	(67.60)%	(14.70)%	0.32%
Difference in ROE (direct vs. indirect)	19.89%	1.50%	0.02%	0.31%
ROA from operations	3.18%	2.19%	2.47%	3.78%

Clearly, shareholders have been losing wealth since FY2015; prior to that the positive returns were too low to matter. It will help to go back a few years more to understand when this process of performance degradation began and how early an analyst could have caught the impending bad news.

The ROE for FY2017 is appallingly low and is a function of not only net losses for the year but also of the very low (but positive) average equity for the year. If this trend were to continue, what would the ROE for FY2018 look like? Believe it or not, it will be a positive number! Why? The numerator and the denominator will both be negative and the resultant quotient will turn positive. *Hence, beyond a point, traditional ratio analysis as a tool loses effectiveness and has to be used and interpreted with care.* The 19.89 percent contribution to ROE from OI is also on account of the very low shareholder equity for the year and cannot be interpreted as impressive performance on that front due to management's efforts. We will, however, focus on the prior 3 years to understand what the numbers tell us.

ROE fell to below 1 percent in FY2014 primarily on account of the interest burden of more than 98 percent, that is, interest expenses for the year were more than 98 percent of the EBIT earned for the year. This has been steadily increasing to beyond 100 percent, making the term

RES in our DuPont framework negative. When RES becomes negative (or interest coverage ratio falls to below 1.0), despite running profitable operations, the firm will post negative ROE as all the operating profits and more are diverted toward servicing debt obligations. This is the situation with Bhushan as well. ROA is positive as a result of a positive NOPAT margin but ROE has turned negative.

However, at single digits, the ROA is not very impressive. From 3.78 percent in FY2014, it dropped to 2.47 percent and 2.19 percent in the following two years before reviving to 3.18 percent in FY2017. While it might be too soon to call the ROA performance poor as we have not compared Bhushan's performance to peers, suffice it to say that any ROA lesser than the average cost of debt for the firm is a recipe for financial distress. A back-of-the-envelope calculation of Bhushan's average interest rate indicates an accelerating trend from 6.5 percent in FY2014 to over 17 percent in FY2017.

While the NOPAT margins of the company seem mediocre, the real culprit for the low ROA seems to be the very low asset utilization indicated by ATR of less than 30 percent for all the years under analysis. Once the analyst has inferred all this, what is the next step?

Depending on the purpose of the analysis, the analyst will be interested in two areas. First, whether the poor performance was due to mismanagement or due to external factors and second, whether this is a trend set to continue and if the firm is indeed going into an irreversible fall. The answer to the first will actually drive the answer to the second question. This will require comparing Bhushan's performance with past years as well as with peers.

Past year data reveal that Bhushan returned its equity holders more than 20 percent (on operations) until FY2010 after which the returns fell dramatically to about 18 percent, 14 percent, and 10 percent in the next 3 years. During these years the firm saw its NOPAT margin actually improving from 12 percent in FY2009 to over 18 percent in FY2011 and beyond. ATR on the contrary slipped from 0.52× to 0.25× from FY2009 to FY2013, impacting ROA. Financial leverage (LEV) consistently declined from over 5× in FY2009 to reach 3.75× in FY2012, only to zoom back up to 5.48× in FY2013. However, this high LEV contributed to improving its ROE without causing financial distress as is evidenced by its manageable interest burden during this period that stood at 38 percent in FY2009 but steadily increased to over 59 percent in FY2013.

Prima facie, this indicates that mismanagement was not an issue. The periods coinciding with the deterioration in performance, that is, FY2012 onwards, is the period when the global financial crisis hit the Indian economy and global commodity prices saw their lowest levels. All steel manufacturing companies were hit by the global commodity price crisis.

Firms like Bhushan were probably in an expansion mode as is indicated by an increase in their total assets during this period. This expansion was financed using high leverage—the usual practice for this sector. This would have been just normal business but for the commodity crisis taking the industry by surprise. Many commodity firms saw a drastic drop in their revenues due to both prices and volumes reducing. It appears that Bhushan was relatively more resilient on this front. However, the dipping ATR clearly indicates that revenues were not keeping up with the growth in assets. Interestingly, Bhushan seems to have managed to not only maintain its operating profit margin quite well during this period but also improve it, probably by cutting costs. So where has the firm gone wrong?

It appears the firm did all it could and needed to do in the face of a crisis caused by sudden external factors. The asset pileup and incidental debt pileup, which were possibly planned in view of past commodity price and volume trends continuing into the future, became the proverbial albatross around their neck. A firm takes on leverage in the hope that the assets created/purchased using the funds will generate sufficient surplus to service the debt. Revenue pressure resulted in low ATR and low EBIT, though the firm managed to keep up its EBIT margins for some years. Low EBIT coupled with high interest costs started hitting the firm's returns starting FY2012 as is evident from their rapidly decreasing interest coverage ratio and dipping ROE.

The reader will recollect from Chapter 2 that leverage brings gains to the shareholder only when the product of the increasing LEV and decreasing RES is greater than unity. As is evident from Table 3.15, Bhushan Steel managed this feat only until FY2013. For FY2014, the firm's ROE was reduced to 6 percent of its ROA and turned negative thereafter. Using shareholder equity to pay off lenders means transfer of wealth from equity holders to debt holders. It is quite possible that the firm raised more debt in order to service its existing debt, pushing it into a debt trap.

Table 3.15 *Impact of financial leverage on ROA*

	For year ended								
	March 2017	March 2016	March 2015	March 2014	March 2013	March 2012	March 2011	March 2010	March 2009
RES × LEV	(177.73)	(19.92)	(4.30)	0.06	2.24	1.82	2.66	3.46	3.13

What are the key learnings from this case? High leverage in itself does not indicate poor financial position, but it definitely increases risk for equity holders. A firm going for high leverage has to have a clear plan for and control over its operations as it is the returns and CFO that will be required to service the debt. The management has to have deep insight into factors that can impact its operations and the extent to which management has control over such factors. The lesser the control, the greater is the expected volatility in operating margins and profits and greater is the possibility and probability of financial distress.

Firms can also respond to surprises that impact operations by raising cash through sale of assets or other arrangements they may have in place. This, in turn, depends on the type of industry the firm belongs to and the asset portfolio it has in place that can be used without affecting long-term sustainability of operations.

The fact that Bhushan Steel runs robust operations is evident from the cash flow statement in Table 3.16 as well. Despite losses before tax, which have been caused due to high interest expenses, its operating cash flows before and after working capital changes are positive. It is creditable for a firm in such a dire financial situation to have maintained its core operations in shape. However, the CFO is decreasing and may soon turn negative unless the firm sees a quick turnaround. That the company was in investment mode even until FY2014 is evident from the high figure against purchase of fixed assets, after which it seems to have been curbed.

Low operating cash flows coupled with high investment outflows reduces free cash flows (FCF). FCF are defined as CFO less capital expenditure (capex). FCF indicate the surplus cash that a firm is able to

Table 3.16 Cash flow statements for Bhushan Steels Ltd.

	For year ended 31st day of				
	March 2017	March 2016	March 2015	March 2014	March 2013
Profit before tax	(41.26)	(41.95)	(12.58)	0.92	12.09
Adjustment	72.64	63.18	34.47	27.41	21.30
CFO before changes in working capital	31.38	21.24	21.89	28.33	33.40
Trade and other receivables	(3.77)	(0.68)	0.48	(1.38)	(11.23)
Inventories	(10.50)	(1.81)	(8.41)	(9.21)	(22.48)
Loans and advances	(4.11)	1.40	1.86	1.95	(3.48)
Trade and other payables	(4.24)	(10.86)	5.91	4.12	3.95
Changes in working capital	(22.61)	(11.94)	(0.16)	(4.52)	(33.25)
Cash flow after changes in W-Cap.	8.77	9.29	21.73	23.81	0.15
Tax paid	(0.02)	(0.05)	(0.01)	(0.78)	(2.26)
Cash from operating activities	8.74	9.24	21.72	23.03	(2.11)
Purchase of fixed assets	(2.52)	(7.14)	(17.20)	(48.76)	(45.28)
Sale of fixed assets	0.01	6.23	3.32	0.04	0.02
Net purchases of investments	(1.22)	(0.53)	0.00	(2.20)	(0.10)
Interest income	0.47	0.61	0.11	0.28	0.15
Other investment activities	1.24	(1.21)	(0.25)	2.42	(0.02)
Cash flow from investing activities	(2.02)	(2.04)	(14.02)	(48.22)	(45.22)
Proceeds from long-term borrowings	(0.19)	20.04	24.23	38.26	46.80
Proceeds from preference shares	0.06	0.65	0.00	0.00	0.00
Redemption of preference shares	(0.29)	(3.87)	(2.22)	(5.14)	(0.14)
Proceeds from issue of equity share	0.00	0.00	2.00	5.37	3.25

Table 3.16 (continued)

	For year ended 31st day of				
	March 2017	March 2016	March 2015	March 2014	March 2013
Equity dividend and tax paid	0.19	0.00	(0.23)	(0.16)	(0.22)
Interest paid	(14.88)	(40.42)	(43.34)	(31.43)	(26.92)
Net movement in other fin activities	9.32	15.95	11.89	17.50	22.46
Cash from financing activities	**(5.79)**	**(7.65)**	**(7.67)**	**24.40**	**45.23**
Net cash inflow/ outflow	0.93	(0.46)	0.03	(0.79)	(2.09)
Opening cash and cash equivalents	0.41	0.87	0.84	1.63	3.72
Closing cash and cash equivalent	1.35	0.41	0.87	0.84	1.63

Note: All amounts are in INR billion.

generate from its operations after providing for required investment in assets for future growth. This cash allows the firm flexibility around contingencies, prepaying outstanding debt, distributing greater dividends, or buying back equity. We include all investment in operating assets including intangibles in this definition of capex.

Bhushan's FCF as shown in Table 3.17 make for interesting analysis. While the firm had been clearly moving into financial distress leading up to insolvency proceedings in FY2017, its FCF were steadily improving since FY2013. Is this good news? Before we react, it is important to understand what has caused this trend. FY2013 saw a combination of negative CFO and high capex. This was followed by positive CFO combined with relatively higher investments in assets. From FY2015 when the commodity price crisis began hurting the industry, CFO has seen a reducing trend. Creditably, the firm contained its capex in FY2015 (or probably the planned capex was already completed) leading to a positive FCF. Positive FCF in FY2016 and FY2017 is not really anything to cheer about as it shows a company in financial trouble trying to salvage resources. CFO dipped to single digits and further capex was not an option.

Table 3.17 Free cash flows for Bhushan Steels Ltd.

	For year ended 31st day of				
	March 2017	March 2016	March 2015	March 2014	March 2013
Cash from operating activities	8.74	9.24	21.72	23.03	(2.11)
Cash flow from investing activities	(2.02)	(2.04)	(14.02)	(48.22)	(45.22)
Free cash flows	6.23	8.33	7.83	(25.69)	(47.36)

Note: All amounts in INR billion.

So how does a firm running negative FCF manage cash resources? When internal cash generation falls short of investment requirements, external sources are tapped. As discussed in Chapter 2, this is quite normal, especially in industries where capex is heavy and gestation periods are long. This can develop into a vicious cycle of financial distress if the investments do not start generating cash soon enough to service these external sources of funding. In the case of Bhushan, we see that during FY2013 and FY2014, fresh long-term borrowings were in sync with capital expenditure (Capex) requirement, whereas in the following two years while capex significantly reduced, borrowings had increased. This supports the possibility that the company may have been borrowing in order to service its existing debt.

Another interesting feature of Bhushan Steel's financials is the negative net working capital (NWC) similar to what we saw for HUL. We had then discussed how maintaining negative NWC seems a strategic choice for HUL and it reflects the firm's strength in the market. Does the same thesis hold for Bhushan Steel? A closer look at the latter's numbers reveals that what signaled strength for HUL in fact, signals weak financial situation for Bhushan. FY2013 shows positive NWC, which then turns into negative in FY2014 and has been consistently dropping in FY2016 and FY2017. Second, the line item(s) that turn the balance for Bhushan are interest expenses and unpaid debt liability. A firm's negative NWC signals its strength when it reflects the firm's bargaining power with its customers and suppliers. In Bhushan's case, the negative NWC has been the result of the debt trap it has got itself into.

Off-the-Balance Sheet Items

Last but not least, we have an off-the-balance-sheet item of Contingent Liabilities for both HUL and Bhushan. Very often this item and similar off-balance-sheet items get ignored as they do not figure in any of the standard ratios of performance, profitability, or distress. For both firms they constitute 12 percent to 13 percent of the balance sheet size. But it is interesting to note the difference in implication for both firms. At 13 percent of total balance sheet size they are not exactly insignificant even for HUL but the fact that they are reducing as a percentage of total assets makes it a less stressful situation as compared to Bhushan's case. For the latter firm, contingent liabilities were just over 2 percent of total assets in FY2013 and have consistently grown to over 12 percent of total assets by FY2017.

In absolute terms, they have risen for both firms but the rate of increase has been far more for Bhushan. Second, Bhushan has seen erosion of shareholder equity and total assets over the last 3 years leading to further acceleration in contingent liabilities as proportion of balance sheet size. It is quite likely that the reasons for increase in contingent liabilities for both firms are different. For HUL the reasons would be regular increase in size of business and number of transactions. On the contrary, for Bhushan it is quite likely that financial distress in the industry and the company may have led to greater disputes and litigations than would have in normal times. The exponential rise in the quantum of contingent liabilities from FY2015 to FY2016 corresponds to steep decline in Bhushan's profits and net worth.

To summarize, the story and the numbers have to move together. A reader of the financial statements has to have a fair idea of the business the firm is in so as to make sense of the numbers in context. The common-size and time-series versions of financial statements are simple yet powerful tools that allow this. Margins, asset compositions, asset productivity, leverage capability—all differ across industry depending on the production process, type of assets used, competition, business strategy, etc. While the stock market is an equalizer—an investor is looking to maximize returns on her investment in any stock and will go for the one offering most attractive risk–return combination—the manner in which each firm achieves this return for the investor, varies. The DuPont analysis is a good place to start as it allows the analyst to disaggregate the ROE into its vital components and identify problem areas. Most importantly, this framework helps segregate business decisions and outcomes from financial decisions and outcomes. It also helps segregate core business activities from the noncore ones and evaluate the contribution of each to total shareholder returns.

CHAPTER 4

Financial Statements of Service Businesses

As seen in Chapter 3, there are fundamental differences in the balance sheet and P&L compositions between goods and services businesses. But not all service businesses resemble Infosys Ltd. Service businesses can be asset heavy and may hold significant amount of inventory too. Then what is the need to study analysis of service firms separately from firms engaged in goods? Are they really different? Producing a "unit of a service" versus a unit of a physical item for sale has quite different impact on costs of production/service for the respective firms. Impact of operating leverage and benefits of scale economies are different for both types of firms as we will see in the examples in this chapter.

Analyzing Asset-Heavy Service Firms

The first example is Bharti Airtel Ltd. (BAL), India's leading telecommunications company. The company provides mobile and fixed line services, tower infrastructure, and is also engaged in tele-media and payments banking. BAL derives over 50 percent of its revenues from mobile services in India and southeast Asia and over 20 percent of revenues from mobile services in Africa.

Table 4.1 lays out the balance sheets for BAL for 5 years[1]. What are some of the initial observations about the firm?

Clearly, the firm has been growing profitably given that it has accumulated reserves in excess of 27 times its invested share capital. Second, the business model of BAL is asset heavy; it has fixed assets at 2.8× its net

---

[1]Financial statements of Bharti Airtel Ltd. have been sourced from the Ace Analyzer database.

Table 4.1 Balance sheets for Bharti Airtel Ltd.

	For year ended 31st day of				
	March 2017	March 2016	March 2015	March 2014	March 2013
Sources of funds					
Share capital incl. warrants	24.05	25.15	21.33	19.64	18.32
Total reserve	650.51	642.54	376.44	577.92	484.90
Shareholder's funds	674.56	667.69	397.77	597.56	503.22
Minority interest	68.75	54.98	68.91	42.10	40.89
Secured loans	7.05	18.76	93.57	98.88	84.41
Unsecured loans	938.26	916.69	579.48	508.33	530.64
Total debts	945.31	935.44	673.05	607.21	615.05
Total liabilities	**1688.63**	**1658.12**	**1139.73**	**1246.87**	**1159.15**
Application of funds					
Fixed assets	2715.18	2596.37	2083.10	2101.96	1849.23
Less: Accumulated depreciation	932.83	873.44	840.32	693.17	559.93
Less: Impairment of assets	0.00	0.00	0.00	2.64	2.64
Net block	1782.35	1722.93	1242.79	1406.15	1286.66
Capital work in progress	108.39	57.02	174.15	0.00	0.00
Investments	224.28	218.15	259.11	201.41	115.74
Total noncurrent assets	2115.01	1998.10	1676.05	1607.55	1402.40
Inventories	0.49	4.40	3.75	1.42	1.11
Sundry debtors	49.84	55.04	52.07	62.44	67.82
Cash and bank	16.18	50.99	20.83	49.81	16.08
Other current assets	81.22	77.21	20.28	37.11	34.03
Loans and advances	38.51	27.47	228.40	10.81	12.32
Total current assets	186.23	215.11	325.34	161.59	131.36
Less: Current Liabilities and Provisions					
Current liabilities	621.14	574.98	638.66	566.33	418.78
Provisions	8.30	14.34	206.64	1.73	1.77
Total current liabilities	629.45	589.32	845.31	568.05	420.55
Net current assets	(443.22)	(374.21)	(519.97)	(406.46)	(289.19)
Deferred tax assets/ liabilities	16.83	34.23	(20.64)	45.78	45.94
Total assets	**1688.63**	**1658.12**	**1135.44**	**1246.87**	**1159.15**
Contingent liabilities	134.82	101.98	205.74	141.84	98.11

Note: Amounts in INR billion.

worth. This is quite unlike what one would expect of a service business. Assets to the tune of 2.8× of net worth also mean BAL has used substantial debt funds to finance its business.

Not only has BAL used high amount of financial leverage, but this has primarily been in the form of unsecured loans. While these characteristics are quite "goods-firms like," a service firm like characteristic is the very small amounts of inventory in BAL's balance sheet.

Cost of (raw) materials is conspicuous by its absence in the P&L statement of BAL in Table 4.2. Bulk of a telecom firm's core service costs comprise expenses of operating the network such as charges for Internet, bandwidth, and leased lines; infrastructure charges including repair and maintenance. Other big-ticket items are access charges as calls move from one service provider's network on to another's, and revenue charges for spectrum and license fees.

Table 4.2 Profit and loss statement for Bharti Airtel Ltd.

| | For year ended 31st day of | | | | |
	March 2017	March 2016	March 2015	March 2014	March 2013
Gross sales	954.68	965.32	961.01	858.64	769.47
Expenditure					
Employee cost	43.03	49.11	48.57	46.23	38.82
Other manufacturing expenses	419.11	419.32	382.39	389.82	360.88
G&A, S&D exp.	116.53	131.05	170.89	137.75	131.92
Miscellaneous expenses	24.03	27.02	23.14	7.06	5.26
Total expenditure	602.70	626.50	624.99	580.87	536.89
EBITDA	351.98	338.82	336.02	277.77	232.58
Depreciation	197.73	174.50	198.58	156.50	148.15
EBIT	154.25	164.32	137.44	121.27	84.43
Other income	19.70	17.20	20.96	10.41	5.10
PBIT	173.95	181.52	158.40	131.68	89.53
Interest	95.47	85.46	44.47	58.79	45.19
Exceptional income/expenses	(11.70)	21.74	(8.53)	0.54	0.00
Profit before tax	66.78	117.80	105.40	73.43	44.35
Provision for tax	34.82	59.53	54.87	48.45	25.18
Profits after tax	31.96	58.26	50.53	24.98	19.16

Note: Amounts in INR billion.

Since the firm has been financed using significant amount of debt funds, interest cost is significant and comprises almost 10 percent of revenues and nearly 62 percent of EBIT for FY2017. It is then important to determine if the debt burden is bearable for the operations of the firm. Our DuPont analysis framework reveals that levels of debt carried by the firm have been eroding shareholder wealth. The ROA of the firm, though not very impressive, is healthy. However, the equity holders are getting a lower return on their investment as the amplifying impact of leverage (high LEV) is getting outweighed by the interest burden (low RES). The product of RES and LEV is less than 1 as seen in the DuPont analysis in Table 4.3.

While it may be premature to comment on a firm's ratios without benchmarking them to industry peers, it is clear that the operating profit margins for BAL have been improving, while the asset utilization has dipped significantly in FY2017. These two opposing forces have kept the ROA more or less steady, limiting improvement to only a percentage point over the 4 years. Hence, it becomes imperative to first investigate what has caused the dip in ATR. At the earlier average ATR of 58 percent, BAL would have clocked an ROA of over 7 percent in FY2017.

The rewards of the ROA have been further diluted by the time they have got translated into ROE. When the interest burden is as high as 80 percent, the leverage (LEV) has to be 5× for the product of RES and LEV to be unity, that is, to simply maintain ROA for equity holders.

Table 4.3 DuPont analysis for Bharti Airtel Ltd.

	For year ended 31st day of			
	March 2017	March 2016	March 2015	March 2014
ROE (direct computation)	4.36%	9.80%	9.13%	4.22%
Interest burden	79.93%	81.56%	53.85%	80.73%
NOPAT margin	12.51%	10.86%	8.59%	8.48%
ATR	0.47	0.52	0.58	0.58
LEV	2.78	3.14	2.99	2.52
ROE (indirect computation)	3.27%	3.25%	6.89%	2.37%
ROA from operations	5.87%	5.61%	4.99%	4.88%
Total impact of leverage	0.56	0.58	1.38	0.49

This seems intuitively incorrect at first glance. When the firm is unable to manage leverage levels of 2.78×, how would it manage a 5× leverage? Indeed, the question to ask is why has interest burden reached 80 percent when it should not have gone beyond 64 percent (calculated as "1 − 1/ 2.78") at the current leverage levels.

Interest burden is a function of two variables—interest expenses and operating profits. At leverage levels of 2.78×, interest expenses should be within 64 percent of operating profits in order to prevent a dilutive impact of financial leverage on ROA upon converting into ROE. 80 percent interest burden reveals that the revenues and profit margins of BAL put together are inadequate for the quantum and cost of debt put together. Our variable RES in the DuPont analysis only accounts for the interest burden on debt. What about the principal repayments? The firm needs to earn sufficient profits to cover these as well.

The Debt Service Coverage Ratio (DSCR) helps gauge this aspect. A step further from the Interest Coverage Ratio (ICR), it measures the extent to which operating profits cover all financing payments including lease rentals, if any. Taking EBITDA as the measure of operating profits as depreciation and amortization are noncash expenses, a simple DSCR[2] shows that BAL is unable to cover its debt servicing commitments completely through its earnings for respective years. The good news is that the ratio has improved over the years and touched 0.95× in FY2017 implying that the EBITDA for the year was sufficient to cover 95 percent of the firm's debt commitments for the year.

The reader will note that here we have four variables—revenues, operating profit margins, debt amount, and cost of debt. The reader may also recollect that in our example of Bhushan Steel Ltd. in the previous chapter, we saw the firm had improved significantly on its profit margins, yet was pushed into insolvency proceedings. This was because the amount of revenues on which the margins were applied was insufficient to bear the load of the debt on the balance sheet and the cost thereof.

---

[2]This is calculated as EBITA divided by sum of interest payments and debt repayments for the year. Since interest expenses are tax deductible while principal repayments are not, every dollar of principal repayment requires $1/(1 − t)$ dollars of pretax profits. This pulls down the DSCR further.

This analysis essentially forces the analyst to think thus. For a firm that has taken a certain amount of debt, has it taken it at a reasonable cost? The other pertinent question is, where is the debt raised being invested? This gets reflected in the assets on the balance sheet. Next is how well are these assets being converted into revenues? This gets reflected in the ATR and finally, how well is the revenue churning out profits, which is explained by the profit margins. In the case of both Bhushan Steel and BAL, it appears that the problem lies in the deployment of the debt raised and/or the utilization of assets. So we take a more detailed look at where BAL has been investing through a study of its cash flow statements in Table 4.4.

Table 4.4 Cash flow statements for Bharti Airtel Ltd.

	For year ended 31st day of				
	March 2017	March 2016	March 2015	March 2014	March 2013
Profit before tax	77.23	128.46	105.40	78.64	47.85
Adjustments	264.58	201.75	226.32	196.40	185.47
Trade and other receivables	13.00	12.66	(18.04)	2.07	(3.82)
Inventories	0.95	(0.87)	(0.00)	(0.15)	0.27
Loans and advances	(54.54)	(21.90)	0.00	0.00	0.00
Trade and other payables	13.17	6.16	16.01	19.33	25.15
Changes in working capital	(27.43)	(3.96)	(2.04)	21.25	21.59
Cash flow after changes in WK	314.39	326.26	329.69	296.30	254.91
Tax and others	(22.08)	(46.84)	(49.10)	(33.97)	(27.21)
Cash from operating activities	292.31	279.42	280.59	262.33	227.70
Purchase of fixed assets	(477.58)	(277.98)	(222.51)	(179.02)	(131.47)
Sale of fixed assets	4.46	3.80	4.61	4.36	1.40
Purchase of investments	0.00	0.00	(3.64)	(30.84)	(56.67)
Sale of investments	95.21	128.23	5.62	0.00	0.00
Other investment activities	62.35	3.69	(7.13)	(44.23)	(0.03)
Cash flow from investing activities	(315.55)	(142.26)	(223.05)	(249.73)	(186.76)

Table 4.4 (continued)

	For year ended 31st day of				
	March 2017	March 2016	March 2015	March 2014	March 2013
Proceeds from long-term borrowings	258.58	187.27	349.83	361.22	257.69
Repayment of long-term borrowings	(274.61)	(309.66)	(433.18)	(348.43)	(274.44)
Short-term loans	25.38	4.56	6.26	1.46	(7.28)
Proceeds from issue of equity	1.25	0.98	0.00	67.96	32.30
Equity dividend paid	(9.17)	(15.30)	(23.47)	(6.74)	(5.54)
Interest paid	(58.57)	(32.89)	(36.51)	(37.62)	(34.34)
Other financial activities	53.62	45.58	40.34	(10.11)	(14.06)
Cash from financing activities	**(3.51)**	**(119.46)**	**(96.72)**	**27.74**	**(45.66)**
Net cash inflow/outflow	**(26.76)**	**17.71**	**(39.19)**	**40.34**	**(4.72)**
Opening cash and cash equivalents	**17.63**	**(1.41)**	**39.58**	**1.31**	**8.04**
Other cash and adj.	(0.76)	1.34	(1.80)	(2.07)	(2.01)
Closing cash and cash equivalent	**(9.88)**	**17.63**	**(1.41)**	**39.58**	**1.31**

Note: Amounts in INR billion.

BAL has clearly been investing ambitiously in fixed assets, especially in FY2017. Besides, they seem to have raised significant amount of funds in the last 2 years through sale of investments. A peek into the composition of assets in the balance sheet will give the analyst an idea of the kind of assets the firm has been investing in. The excerpt from the balance sheets provided in Table 4.5 details out the noncurrent assets of the firm.

While technology and license fees are the largest components, the firm has a significant amount of goodwill on its balance sheet. Goodwill arises when the firm acquires another firm for a value greater than the sum of the fair value of the latter's assets. For example, if BAL acquired a firm for INR 30 billion whose assets are worth INR 20 billion on fair value basis at the time of acquisition, INR 10 billion will appear as goodwill in BAL's books. Essentially, BAL has paid an extra INR 10 billion for intangibles that carry value for business but do not appear on the

Table 4.5 Non-current assets of Bharti Airtel Ltd.

	For year ended 31st day of				
	March 2017	March 2016	March 2015	March 2014	March 2013
Net block	1,782.35	1,722.93	1,242.79	1,406.15	1,286.66
Goodwill	338.08	428.38	247.78	469.14	412.42
Buildings/premises	10.03	12.59	16.93	17.91	15.80
Plant and machinery	596.37	579.21	659.56	538.05	576.18
Furniture, fixtures, office appliances	3.14	3.59	14.02	17.07	17.93
Computer software	20.88	18.75	15.09	13.88	12.56
Technology license fees	797.91	663.19	286.74	218.28	221.45
Other fixed assets	15.95	17.22	2.67	131.83	30.32
Capital work in progress	108.39	57.02	174.15	0.00	0.00
Investments	224.28	218.15	259.11	201.41	115.74
Total noncurrent assets	2,115.01	1,998.10	1,676.05	1,607.55	1,402.40

Note: Amounts in INR billion.

balance sheet, such as customer base, brand, reputation, vendor network, etc. Therefore, these are assets that the acquirer seeks to leverage and earn upon in future.

Unlike other intangible assets, goodwill is not amortized but impaired or written down. This is because goodwill does not endow on the acquirer any definite benefit over an estimable period that purchase of other intangibles like patents or software does. Goodwill is based on the acquirer's sense of worth of *intangibles that do not appear on the balance sheet* of the acquired firm! Hence, when the acquirer firm senses that either the benefits accruing on account of such intangibles have dissipated or the firm is unable to leverage these benefits as it had estimated, it writes the value of goodwill down in its books.

ATR of BAL on assets excluding goodwill works out to 0.58× and 0.63× for FY2017 and FY2016, respectively. A conservative analyst will question the need to do this. Goodwill can be seen as any other asset that was purchased using the firm's financial resources in expectation of value generation in future periods; the "vendors" in this case happen to be the equity (and debt) -holders of the target firm. Much of the goodwill in BAL's books is on account of acquisitions made by the company in Africa. During

FY2017, the company sold some of its subsidiaries/tower operations, which resulted in the reduction of some amount of goodwill carried in its books. This is evident from the CFS too under the head "Sale of Investments."

A further refinement would be to exclude capital work in progress too as these are assets that have not yet been commissioned for operations. However, funds have already been utilized and are in the process of further utilization until these assets can be commissioned. This is a feature of firms that are in businesses with medium to long gestation periods. There is a time lag between investments and them translating into returns and it is important for an analyst to be conscious of this fact and not jump into doomsday conclusions.

We had discussed the concept and significance of free cash flows in the case of Bhushan Steel. BAL's FCF look as in Table 4.6.

Notice that BAL has had a healthy run of FCF in that, they've been positive in all years except in FY2017. However, the trend is clearly a declining one and this can be attributed to increasing capex year on year. This is a better situation than if FCF were declining owing to declining operating cash flows. Much of BAL's investment over these years has been in spectrum and related license fees. Telecom companies purchase spectrum via competitive bidding in auctions held by the government. So the timing of such investment is not completely in the control of the firms themselves. So long as investors see a growing market to deploy these investments and sufficient returns from them, they do not mind negative FCF; not even funding part of the dividends to shareholders, as in the most recent 2 years!

So what is the story emerging from just a study of BAL's financial statements? BAL is one of the largest telecom operators in India and has fair financials as indicated by growing revenues, profitable operations

Table 4.6 Free cash flows of Bharti Airtel Ltd.

	For year ended 31st day of				
	March 2017	March 2016	March 2015	March 2014	March 2013
FCF before dividends	(180.81)	5.24	62.69	87.67	97.64
FCF after dividends	(189.98)	(10.07)	39.22	80.93	92.10

Note: Amounts in INR billion.

despite high interest expenses, and positive operating cash flows and free cash flows. However, the not-so-good news is that the profit margins are meager; in the 5 years under study, the maximum net profit margin the firm has seen is 6 percent in FY2016. The firm is highly leveraged and the operating profits are insufficient to carry its debt servicing burden. Hence, the firm is raising external funds either in the form of equity (see FY2013 and FY2014) and/or debt (all the years) to manage the deficit. An astute reader will see an apparent dichotomy in this argument—while EBITDA may be falling short of debt commitments, is the firm short of cash? EBITDA is not all cash. To resolve this argument, we look at the FCF. While BAL has been posting positive FCF in the first 3 years of our example, this has been far short of the debt commitments, including interest payments. Seen either way, the firm has had to resort to external funds to manage its debt commitments. The investments in assets undertaken over these years need to translate into higher revenues and operating profit margins to improve debt coverage ratios. This should also translate into higher cash flow from operations. Companies normally slow down their capex after a point thereby, releasing further free cash.

The reader should understand that a complete picture can be obtained only by benchmarking to peers and industry as well as verifying and/or strengthening these insights with other qualitative information. We will now look at the financials of a competitor to BAL to understand how two firms in the same industry can be quite different. This is the upstart in the industry—Reliance Jio Infocomm (Jio)[3]—promoted by India's largest private sector company, Reliance Industries Ltd. Jio is an interesting case study; it has attempted to disrupt the telecom market in India and dislodge the leaders, riding on the deep pockets of its parent.

Analyzing the Financials of an Asset-Heavy Start-Up Firm

What strikes most about the numbers displayed in Table 4.7 is the sheer range. In terms of capital and funding and total investments, Jio is a large player. Cash balances and fixed asset investments are small in comparison

---

[3]Financial statements of Reliance Jio Infocomm Private Ltd. have been sourced from the annual reports of its parent company Reliance Ltd.

Table 4.7 Balance sheets of Reliance Jio Infocomm Ltd.

	For year ended 31st day of		
	March 2017	March 2016	March 2015
Sources of funds			
Share capital	518,570	451,250	301,250
Equity—paid up	450,000	450,000	300,000
Convertible pref. shares	68,570	1,250	1,250
Reserves and surplus	190,074	(78,892)	(78,735)
Securities premium	269,280	–	–
Profit and loss account balance	(79,206)	(78,892)	(78,735)
Shareholder's funds	708,644	372,358	222,515
Secured loans	138,352	90,064	15,117
Unsecured loans and liabilities	537,630	371,166	261,034
Total debt	675,982	461,229	276,151
Total liabilities	**1,384,626**	**833,587**	**498,666**
Application of funds			
Gross block	13,606	11,825	10,256
Less: Accumulated depreciation	3,862	2,428	1,398
Net block	9,744	9,397	8,858
Capital work in progress	1,779,776	1,060,720	602,958
Investments	45,780	87,320	50,200
Total noncurrent assets	1,835,300	1,157,437	662,015
Sundry debtors	0.2	0.1	0.3
Cash and bank	268	122	238
Other current assets	4,279	3,191	9,013
Loans and advances	127,135	73,341	28,332
Total current assets	131,682	76,654	37,583
Less: Current liabilities and provisions			
Sundry creditors	461,914	377,778	190,798
Unearned revenue/customer advances	19,470	151	0
Current portion and interest accrued	48,591	17,051	39,920
Other liabilities	93,601	46,862	11,687
Provisions	683	399	182
Total current liabilities	624,258	442,241	242,587
Net current assets	(492,576)	(365,587)	(205,003)
Deferred tax assets/liabilities	41,902	41,737	41,654
Total assets	**1,384,626**	**833,587**	**498,666**

Note: All amounts in INR million.

but capital WIP indicates a very ambitious entrant with huge investments in the pipeline. The range of numbers becomes starker when we see the P&L statement of the firm for FY2016 and FY2017 in Table 4.8.

The revenues for the 2 years of operations are miniscule compared to the balance sheet size as well as the expenses incurred. Clearly, the firm is in its first phase of operations where the scale of operations is still too small to cover its fixed costs. On the other hand, Jio has invested at a massive scale unlike a regular start-up. To put this in perspective, the net capex of Jio for FY2017 is INR 385 billion as against INR 473 billion for the much seasoned BAL. According to the annual report of the parent for the year ended March 31, 2016, RIL—the parent company—has acquired spectrum in the 800 MHz and 2,300 MHz bands across circles to become the only operator with pan-India LTE spectrum in both the

Table 4.8 *Profit and loss statement for Reliance Jio Infocomm Ltd.*

	For year ended 31st day of	
	March 2017	March 2016
Net sales	0.20	0.40
Expenditure		
Employee cost	60.40	40.80
Cost of software developments	17.20	16.00
Operating expenses	3.70	6.80
General and administration expenses	163.80	103.20
Selling and marketing expenses	178.80	37.60
Miscellaneous expenses	8.50	10.50
Total expenditure	43.24	21.49
EBITDA	(4.30)	(2.11)
Depreciation	48.70	43.30
EBIT	(5.30)	(4.54)
Other income	12.00	32.20
PBIT	0.67	2.77
Interest	10.20	14.30
PBT	(0.95)	(1.15)
Provision for tax	(165.40)	(82.80)
Profits after tax	16.44	8.16
Appropriations	(79,206.10)	(78,892.40)

Note: All amounts in INR million.

bands. This is besides the 1,800 MHz band RIL already has in 18 circles. With Jio, RIL has planned to offer an entire platter of solutions across the digital value chain including education, health care, and entertainment. Not only has the firm invested heavily in assets but also in marketing and operations as evidenced by its administration and marketing expenses, respectively.

The magnitude and pattern of investment in operations is also evident from the working capital items in Jio's balance sheet. While sundry debtors are well less than a million, sundry creditors at the end of FY2017 stood at over INR 93 billion! Customer advances are significant, so are other liabilities. Within current assets the largest item is loans and advances. Why would a start-up that has barely begun booking revenues extend loans and advances on such a massive scale?

Let us look at each of the issues one by one.

The P&L statement shows interest expenses of INR 14 and 10 million, respectively, for the 2 years as against overall revenues of less than a million rupees. These interest expenses are only a part of the overall interest liability of Jio on the INR 676 billion of loans and INR 68 billion on preference shares outstanding. As per the firm's annual report, the capital WIP includes project development expenditures capitalized of over INR 900 billion, of which over INR 70 billion are capitalization[4] of interest expenses alone. What would a DuPont analysis on Jio look like at this point? Will it even make sense? It is more important for the reader to think about why a company would capitalize its expenses undertaken during construction and what the pros and cons of such an approach could be.

The matching principle on which accrual accounting system rests demands that expenses be matched to revenues and be booked in the period in which the corresponding revenue is booked. The preoperative period is one where expenses are incurred for revenues to be earned in future. Therefore, in the spirit of the matching principle, it makes sense to capitalize such expenses (we have a zero revenue P&L statement essentially) until the time that the assets are capable of earning revenues.

---

[4]When assets are still in the process of being created, firms are allowed to capitalize revenue expenses incurred thereon, including borrowing costs until such time as the assets reach a stage where they can be put into operation.

In the postoperative periods, these capitalized expenses that are now part of the book values of the respective assets or appear in the balance sheet as miscellaneous expenditure/preoperative expenses not written off, will get depreciated/amortized/written off, as the case may be against these future period revenues.

The current liabilities of Jio under the heads of sundry creditors and other liabilities have accelerated over the 3 years. A closer look at the notes to accounts reveals that all these are amounts owed to suppliers of capital expenditure and to the government for spectrum. Therefore, as against common understanding of payables, Jio's debt is completely on account of capex.

Telecom firms work on a subscriber model where subscribers to their voice, data, and other services either pay in advance or in arrears. To the extent the firm has "prepaid" subscriptions, there appears in their balance sheet an item of unearned revenues or customer advances on the liabilities side of the balance sheet. An accelerated rise in this item indicates high growth in such subscriptions. Essentially, the subscription payments are divided into current revenues (appearing in the P&L statement) and unearned revenues (appearing in the balance sheet). How the firm divides its subscriptions into these two parts is crucial to how the performance story unfolds. Principles of accounting say that the revenue should be earned over the life of the subscription, that is, over the period the subscription provides service to the customer. In businesses where the subscription payments are for a definite number of services or offerings (magazines, newspapers) or definite time period (club membership), this division is straightforward. But in others where utilization cannot be clearly defined[5] it will need estimating based on business model, nature of the offering and customer habits. This split is very interesting in the case of Jio. For the year ended March 31, 2017, while the current revenues are only INR 0.2 million, the unearned portion of the revenues is close to INR 20 billion! It is as if the firm will "earn" practically all its subscription receipts in the future. This is where Jio's business model at least in the

---

[5]In the case of telecom services, it may not be very complicated as usage can be transparently monitored. In the case of some others, such as Internet gaming, warranties, implicit promise of upgrades, etc., ambiguity seeps into the estimation of services rendered, and hence, revenues earned.

years FY2016 and FY2017 was unique as it entered the Indian telecom model with a clear mandate to disrupt traditional business models.

Commencing services in September 2016, Jio on-boarded 100 million subscribers in a mere 170 days by offering free voice services across the country and lowest data tariffs and became the world's largest mobile data carrier. A "Jio Prime" customer got free voice services and all data and apps services for a nominal charge of INR 309 per month for 12 months. In addition, the offer carried a complimentary access to all Jio apps for free until March 31, 2018. From the numbers reported in the annual report, clearly, most subscribers went the "prepaid" route. Until March 31, 2017, only a miniscule portion of the services against the subscriptions were delivered and hence, revenues "earned." One would expect to see much of this unearned revenue getting realized in the financial years ending March 31, 2018 and 2019. However, the firm carries liability on account of the rest of the amount collected in terms of service delivery.

Earlier in this section we had observed that the scale of capital expenditure Jio had been undertaking was only marginally lower than that of the market leader, BAL. What would this mean for an investor or any other stakeholder? Let's compare the two firms on some basic parameters as laid out by the DuPont model. This is shown in Table 4.9.

In terms of balance sheet size and parameters, Jio is almost at par with BAL, carrying almost similar financial leverage (preference share capital is classified as debt in Table 4.9 in line with IFRS) but very much a start-up when it comes to its operations. Clearly, Jio has managed this scale only because of the deep pockets of its parent. The positive PAT despite the

Table 4.9 DuPont parameters

FY2017	BAL	Jio
Total assets	1,688.63	1,384.63
Capex	473.12	385.40
Total debt	945.31	744.55
Total equity	674.56	640.07
Revenues	954.68	0.0002
EBIT	154.25	(0.01)
PAT	31.96	0.02

Note: All amounts in INR billion.

operating loss is the result of income tax credits on losses and deferred tax adjustments carried forward. The real question is the revenues and profits it would take for Jio to break even given the massive scale of investment and debt it has taken on.

The reader will recollect from the previous section that BAL's ROA was being driven by its profit margins and its ATR needed improving. For Jio to even manage an equivalent ATR of 0.66 means it needs revenues of INR 914 billion. We can make a reasonable assumption that attaining close enough operating profit margins may not be such a challenge if economies of scale kick in. However, for the ROA to convert into ROE without dilution for shareholders, the financial leverage aspect has to be managed. The leverage (LEV) indicated by Table 4.9 is 2.16×. This means Jio needs an ICR of 1.86×[6] to simply ensure ROA conservation. Taking the current interest expense run rate including the part Jio has capitalized that will in future appear as revenue expenses, we can work with an interest expense of INR 70 billion (the CFS indicates payments on account of interest at over INR 58 billion in FY2017). This gives us a required EBIT of INR 130 billion. This translates to a 14.2 percent pretax operating profit margin on the breakeven revenues of INR 914 billion, that is, a pretax ROA of 9.4 percent. In a nutshell, what we can see is a challenging scenario for the ambitious Jio to come up with market pacifying returns!

The DuPont framework can, thus, be used not only to separate out the historical performance metrics of a business but also to work backwards to the *required* metrics for a firm to achieve a certain state such as operating breakeven or a certain required ROE for equity holders.

Analyzing an Asset-Light Services Business

India is famous for its information technology (IT) outsourcing industry that created giants such as Tata Consultancy Services (TCS) Ltd., Infosys Ltd., etc. This industry was instrumental in changing demographics and cultural behavior, not to mention being a large creator of employment and source of export revenues for the country. This industry is today at a

---

[6] To just prevent ROA dilution, we need RES × LEV to be unity, that is, RES of 0.46. RES = 1 − 1/ICR.

turning point where its *cash-cow©* is losing steam and it needs to reinvent itself and find new *stars©* that will propel its growth in the future. An IT outsourcing firm can be started "in the garage" as many Silicon Valley legends began and requires low investment in fixed assets. These assets primarily comprise computer hardware, servers, furniture and fixtures as we saw in the common-size version of the financial statements of Infosys Ltd. in Chapter 2. We will now dig deeper into the business model of an IT company using the financial statements of TCS Ltd[7].

The key observations from the balance sheet in Table 4.10 can be summarized thus:

1. The business uses more current assets than noncurrent assets for operations. Of the latter, investments are the largest component. The reader will do well to recollect that investments are nonoperating in nature.
2. Within current assets sundry debtors or receivables from clients is the single largest item—a clear indication of the "services" nature of the business (in a goods-based business, typically inventory will be the largest current asset or at least equally large).
3. On the financing side, equity financing clearly dominates long-term funding. Current liabilities too are a significant source of finance, in line with current assets. Current assets and liabilities vary with the level of operations of a firm.

What can one infer about the IT outsourcing business from just these observations? First, that this business is driven more by human capital than fixed capital assets. Second, the balance sheet size is more corre-lated with current scale of business than for companies such as Bhushan or BAL. This is because current assets, which move more in sync with revenues and current operations, dominate the assets side of the balance sheet for TCS. For a firm engaged in metals and mining or a telecom-munications company, fixed assets are put in place keeping in view scale of operations for the next many years. Therefore, the need for long dura-tion funding is also limited in the case of TCS as is evident by negligible

---

[7]Financial statements of TCS Ltd. have been sourced from the Ace Analyzer database.

Table 4.10 Balance sheets for TCS Ltd.

	As on 31st day of				
	March 2017	March 2016	March 2015	March 2014	March 2013
Sources of funds					
Share capital	1.97	1.97	1.96	1.96	2.96
Reserves and surplus	860.17	708.75	504.39	489.99	383.50
Shareholder's funds	862.14	710.72	506.35	491.95	386.46
Minority interest	3.66	3.55	11.28	7.08	6.95
Secured loans	0.71	0.83	1.14	1.26	1.29
Unsecured loans	13.97	14.42	11.23	11.30	7.97
Total debts	14.68	15.25	12.37	12.56	9.27
Total liabilities	880.48	729.52	530.00	511.59	402.68
Application of funds					
Gross block	229.88	215.86	194.09	161.66	152.04
Less: Accumulated depreciation	112.87	98.12	77.71	66.22	53.76
Net block	117.01	117.74	116.38	95.44	98.28
Capital work in progress	15.41	16.70	27.66	31.68	18.95
Investments	485.19	322.40	113.42	122.66	96.65
Total noncurrent assets	617.61	456.84	257.47	249.79	213.88
Inventories	0.21	0.16	0.16	0.15	0.21
Sundry debtors	226.84	240.73	204.38	182.30	140.96
Cash and bank	41.49	67.88	185.56	144.42	67.69
Other current assets	86.99	65.77	63.52	65.87	50.81
Loans and advances	33.37	32.80	19.58	24.65	45.03
Total current assets	388.90	407.34	473.20	417.39	304.69
Less: Current liabilities and provisions					
Current liabilities	125.84	138.19	126.63	92.84	74.31
Provisions	19.28	17.50	76.55	63.86	42.33
Total current liabilities	145.12	155.69	203.18	156.70	116.65
Net current assets	243.78	251.65	270.02	260.69	188.05
Deferred tax assets/liabilities	19.09	21.03	2.51	1.11	74.74
Total assets	880.48	729.52	530.00	511.59	402.68

Note: All amounts are in INR billion.

amount of long-term debt on its balance sheet. Hence, one can expect low financial leverage unless we include current liabilities as debt, and interest expenses to be very low. Also, asset utilization as measured by ATR can be very high for such firms if their current assets are well managed.

Table 4.11 Profit and loss statements for TCS Ltd.

	For year ended 31st day of				
	March 2017	March 2016	March 2015	March 2014	March 2013
Net sales	1,179.66	1,086.46	946.48	818.09	629.89
Expenditure					
Employee cost	616.21	553.48	509.24	404.86	319.22
Software dev. costs	28.08	25.71	38.36	30.89	26.53
Other operating expenses	212.26	200.50	154.06	130.88	103.76
Total expenditure	856.55	779.69	701.67	566.62	449.50
EBITDA	**323.11**	**306.77**	**244.82**	**251.47**	**180.40**
Depreciation	19.87	18.88	17.99	13.49	10.80
EBIT	**303.24**	**287.89**	**226.83**	**237.98**	**169.60**
Other income	42.21	30.84	32.30	16.43	11.78
PBIT	**345.45**	**318.73**	**259.13**	**254.40**	**181.38**
Interest	0.32	0.33	1.04	0.39	0.48
Except. income/expenses	0.00	0.00	4.90	0.00	0.00
Profit before tax	**345.13**	**318.40**	**262.98**	**254.02**	**180.90**
Provision for tax	81.56	75.02	62.39	60.70	40.14
Profits after tax	**263.57**	**243.38**	**200.60**	**193.32**	**140.76**

Note: All amounts are in INR billion.

Since these firms are driven more by human capital, one can expect employee cost to be high and a key driver of margins. Let us now turn to their P&L statement (See Table 4.11) to verify some of our propositions.

As expected, employee costs comprise over 70 percent of all operating expenses and account for over 50 percent of total revenues for the company. This means that for such businesses, recruitment, staffing, fitment, and compensation become key drivers of revenues and profitability, implying a key role for the human resources function. Expenses on account of depreciation and interest are very low on account of low levels of fixed assets and debt financing, respectively. This means that such firms are able to convert practically all of their EBITDA into profits before taxes. So we have a combination of high profit margins, high ATR, and low leverage. What might this mean for ROA and ROE of such firms? To find out, let us run through a DuPont analysis for TCS in Table 4.12.

TCS is a firm that has been posting healthy profit margins and high ATR resulting in high ROA that crossed 40 percent in FY2017. However,

Table 4.12 DuPont analysis for TCS Ltd.

	For year ended 31st day of			
	March 2017	March 2016	March 2015	March 2014
ROE (direct computation)	33.36%	39.51%	39.46%	43.32%
Interest burden	0.14%	0.16%	0.63%	0.22%
NOPAT margin	18.79%	19.59%	17.37%	21.67%
ATR	2.22	1.87	1.63	1.69
LEV	0.67	0.94	1.14	1.08
ROE (indirect computation)	28.02%	34.51%	32.15%	39.64%
Difference in ROE (direct vs. indirect)	5.34%	5.01%	7.32%	3.68%
ROA from operations	41.70%	36.73%	28.31%	36.69%

as per our analysis presented in Table 4.12, the latest 2 years seem to have seen an erosion of ROA when getting translated into ROE for equity holders. TCS does not suffer from the perils of high leverage leading to high interest burden causing a less than unity value of RES × LEV. In fact, TCS seems to be suffering from a different problem—financial leverage less than unity. But how is this possible when we have measured total assets on a gross basis?

The problem lies in the composition of the gross assets and its breakup into operating and nonoperating assets. TCS holds significant amount of nonoperating investments thereby, reducing the amount of operating assets to below the level of equity. Figure 4.1 will help understand how such a combination of assets results in dilution of returns for the shareholder.

As per good practices of asset financing, TCS is using long-term sources of finance namely, equity and long-term debt to fund its noncurrent assets and the permanent portion of its current assets. However, the noncurrent assets largely comprise investments—investments are more than three times fixed assets—which are funded by expensive equity. But how do we explain the phenomenon here and tie it to what the company is doing?

Investments comprise 47 percent of TCS' total assets, while shareholder equity comprises 84 percent of their total financing. The total equity capital at the end of FY2017 is INR 866 billion as against operating assets of only INR 540 billion. Besides the equity capital, long-term and

Liabilities	Assets
Long term debt = 14.68 = 1.4%	Fixed assets = 151.51 = 14.7%
Equity = 865.80 = 84.4%	Investments = 485.19 = 47.3%
	Current Assets = 388.90 = 38%
Current Liabilities = 145.12 = 14.2%	

Figure 4.1 Balance sheet composition of
TCS as on March 31, 2017

current liabilities amounting to INR 160 billion, are also deployed partly or fully to fund this INR 540 million of operating assets. In other words, there is gross "over-financing" if looked at purely from an operations point of view. With average operating assets for FY2017 being only 67 percent of the total equity funds, the LEV on operations is only 0.67. Any return on these operating assets will accrue to the equity holders only to the extent of this fraction. It has immensely helped TCS that its debt funding is very low and interest burden is negligible. An RES of 0.14 percent almost completely preserves the LEV factor of 0.67. Hence, a 41.70 percent ROA translates into a much lower 28.02 percent ROE. It is another matter altogether that TCS has been posting impressive ROA and a 28 percent ROE is nothing to complain about. It will be interesting to look at what these huge financial investments of TCS are earning its shareholders.

As seen in the case of HUL in the last chapter, returns from financial investments for TCS Ltd. seen in Table 4.13 have been decreasing over the last few years due to decrease in base interest rates and are not expected to pick up much from these levels. Some questions that need asking and answering at this juncture are as follows.

1. For a firm that has operating assets yielding over 40 percent return, how does the market view investment of shareholder funds

in financial assets that are yielding returns as low as 10 percent and 15 percent?

2. If not financial investments, what other avenues of investment would the market prefer the firm chased?

3. Looking at the ROA posted by TCS over the 4 years, ROA of 42 percent in FY2017 seems an outlier. Is it really an outlier or the beginning of a trend? What factors might help answer this question?

Large Indian players in the IT services sector have been operating at high margins and generating reasonable amount of free cash flows (see cash flow statement in Table 4.14 for surplus of CFO over net capex for each year) that have not been deployed into operating assets at a similar rate, resulting in accumulation of funds. These have typically been parked

Table 4.13 ROE generated by financial investments at TCS Ltd.

	For year ended 31st day of			
	March 2017	March 2016	March 2015	March 2014
OI/average investments	10.45%	14.15%	27.36%	14.98%
LEV	0.51	0.35	0.23	0.25
ROE from OI	5.34%	5.01%	6.35%	3.68%

Table 4.14 Cash flow statements for TCS Ltd.

	For year ended 31st day of				
	March 2017	March 2016	March 2015	March 2014	March 2013
Profit before tax	345.13	318.40	262.99	254.01	180.89
Adjustments	(7.13)	(2.10)	(1.97)	(1.56)	1.14
CFO before changes in WK	338.00	316.30	261.03	252.45	182.02
Trade and other receivables	6.80	(29.36)	(21.58)	(40.16)	(26.23)
Inventories	(1.42)	(0.12)	(0.01)	0.06	(0.03)
Loans and advances	(9.59)	(8.49)	(4.99)	(11.08)	(14.51)
Trade and other payables	(2.10)	(11.47)	34.05	16.67	23.10
Changes in working capital	(6.31)	(49.44)	7.47	(34.51)	(17.67)

Table 4.14 (continued)

	For year ended 31st day of				
	March 2017	March 2016	March 2015	March 2014	March 2013
CFO after changes in WK	331.69	266.86	268.50	217.94	164.36
Tax paid	(79.46)	(75.78)	(74.82)	(70.44)	(48.22)
Cash from operating activities	252.23	191.08	193.68	147.51	116.14
Purchase of fixed assets	(19.90)	(19.90)	(29.49)	(31.26)	(26.38)
Sale of fixed assets	0.37	0.22	0.07	0.14	0.05
Purchase of investment	(1,214.25)	(1,173.73)	(672.96)	(826.13)	(287.39)
Sale of investments	1,032.38	1,138.24	693.61	813.27	282.18
Investment in subsi./JVs	0.00	0.00	(2.64)	(4.52)	(1.63)
Interest and dividend income	17.89	18.27	20.04	13.77	8.05
Intercorporate deposits	16.19	(14.60)	1.55	8.75	(27.51)
Other investment activities	0.00	0.00	(27.19)	(70.67)	(8.24)
Cash flow from investing activities	(167.32)	(51.50)	(17.01)	(96.67)	(60.86)
Net change in long-term borrowings	(0.66)	(0.60)	(0.00)	(0.24)	(0.01)
Short-term loans	0.87	(0.73)	0.43	0.08	0.80
Equity dividend w+ tax paid	(109.73)	(95.15)	(170.20)	(54.80)	(57.03)
Interest paid	(0.20)	(0.20)	(1.05)	(0.38)	(0.48)
Other financial activities	(0.54)	0.02	(0.85)	(1.40)	(0.57)
Cash from financing activities	(110.26)	(96.66)	(171.68)	(56.73)	(57.29)
Net cash inflow/outflow	(25.35)	42.92	4.99	(5.90)	(2.01)
Opening cash and equivalents	62.92	18.60	14.66	18.40	19.93
Effect of forex fluctuations	(1.63)	1.40	(1.06)	2.15	0.48
Closing cash and equivalents	35.94	62.92	18.60	14.66	18.40

Note: Amounts in INR billion.

in financial investments yielding far lower returns. In the year 2016, one such IT firm Cognizant Technologies received a rap on its knuckles from activist investor Elliot Management Corp. when the latter questioned the company on its practice of reinvesting surplus funds in avenues that yielded mediocre returns. The reader will understand here that it is not just financial investments that can be questioned. Even operating assets that yield less than acceptable margins erode shareholder returns due to their contribution to lower ROA and consequently lower ROE.

Following the noise over Cognizant's investment strategy, Indian firms, mainly TCS and Infosys, felt pressure from the market to refocus on surplus funds that were a drag on ROE. Since then, TCS and Infosys announced huge share buybacks for their investors, which were well received by the market. A share buyback provides the choice to the shareholder to either keep her funds with the company or to pull it out if she thinks she has more lucrative avenues for deployment. As for the company, it reduces the equity base, thereby increasing the equity multiplier or LEV, and hence increasing ROE. It is important to remember here that such a buyback will have no impact on ROA as the assumption is that these funds are surplus and hence their outflow will have no impact on current operations.

As compared to all the companies analyzed thus far, the reader will notice that in the case of TCS the gap between PBT and EBITDA and between EBITDA and CFO before working capital changes is among the lowest. Cash flows after adjustments or EBITDA is almost 100 percent of PBT indicating the miniscule depreciation and interest expenses components in such a business. CFO after working capital changes range anywhere between 84 percent and 103 percent of EBITDA across the 5 years under study. This implies that working capital movements have been ranging within a narrow 19 percent band of EBITDA. The large difference comes when income taxes are introduced—CFO after taxes account for anywhere between 24 to 30 percentage points of EBITDA!

HUL's corresponding ratios are actually not very different—anywhere between 60 percent and 85 percent of its EBITDA converted into cash flows from operations over the 5 years and taxes accounted for anywhere between 25 percent and 35 percent of this gap. In other words, but for income taxes, CFO accounted for 95 percent to 110 percent of EBITDA for HUL, which is an impressive ratio. So what is different between the operating cash flows of an FMCG firm like HUL and an IT service firm like TCS? In fact, not much. Both are low on financial leverage and fixed assets as a percentage of total balance sheet size leading to low interest and depreciation charges. The difference is actually in working capital composition as we have already seen. However, the *change in working capital* is quite low for both firms as they are both mature in their respective businesses, growing at a steady clip. In fact a look at both firms' investment and financing cash flows also show similar patterns. Their investment into fixed assets is not too high—around 2 percent to 4 percent of gross sales—indicating normal business and no major expansion plans. Purchase and sale of financial investments are huge by comparison in both firms but in net terms almost cancel out. The turnover in financial investments is 90 percent to 101 percent of annual revenues from operations for both firms in FY2017 wherein this ratio was in the vicinity of 45 percent to 55 percent range for FY2013 for both. Clearly, both have been having very healthy free cash flows probably leading to greater activity in the treasury department! In the financing cash flows department, dividends are the one major item for both and this is no surprise having discussed their performance in detail.

However, there is one area where there is a significant difference between what both the firms have been doing, which is not apparent at first look. Let us observe the set of numbers in Table 4.15.

Table 4.15 Analysis of capital expenditure

	For year ended 31st day of				
	March 2017	March 2016	March 2015	March 2014	March 2013
HUL					
Net capital expenditure	(14.52)	(7.72)	(5.73)	(5.84)	(4.41)
Depreciation charges	4.32	3.53	3.22	2.95	2.51
Growth capex	(10.20)	(4.19)	(2.51)	(2.90)	(1.90)
TCS					
Net capital expenditure	(19.53)	(19.68)	(29.43)	(31.12)	(26.33)
Depreciation charges	19.87	18.88	17.99	13.49	10.80
Growth capex	0.34	(0.80)	(11.44)	(17.63)	(15.53)

Note: Amounts in INR billion.

What can one decipher from the trend in capital expenditures for both firms besides what has already been mentioned earlier? HUL's capex has been increasing steadily with FY2017 seeing a big jump, while TCS has seen a consistent decline in net capex since FY2015. What is the significance of comparing capex to depreciation charges? Firms need to replace assets to the extent they depreciate in a year to simply maintain operations at the same level. This is called maintenance capex. However, firms that are planning future growth will have an additional layer of capex that is termed growth capex. TCS has been seeing declining growth capex with FY2017 showing capex less than even maintenance levels! Normally, this would be a reason for concern for equity investors who need to see future growth in operations for value of their investment in the firm to increase. Such a trend could mean that the firms either do not have any growth plans or are seeing a resource crunch such as Bhushan Steel. Resources are definitely not an issue for TCS, so is it the other case then? Before jumping to any conclusions it will help to take a look at the components of fixed (and intangible) assets the firm has been holding on its balance sheet across the years.

Gross block levels of most fixed assets have either increased marginally or remained at the same level, while the depreciation charged on them has been higher. However, goodwill has been declining each year probably driving this trend. However, that is not consolation enough as it still does not show a firm plan on the part of the company to invest into newer technologies or expansion. This was one of the reasons investors were getting restless and the share buyback was welcomed by the market. Of course, the company was returning cash to shareholders by way of dividends but this was far too less compared to the cash flows lying unutilized.

With the analysis of TCS, we have moved from simply looking at profitability or current returns of a firm to what its financial statements portend for the future. This is imperative for both the equity and debt investor to be able to see as they rely on future cash flows for their returns.

CHAPTER 5

Financial Statements of Financial Services Firms

Why should banks and firms offering financial services be discussed separately from other service firms that we saw in the previous chapter? For all firms that we have studied so far, money is a means to procure assets—both fixed assets and current assets—that the firms deploy for their operations. Money is used to procure raw materials that are converted into goods that are further sold to customers to earn revenues and profits. What if money itself becomes the raw material? Well, that's what business models of banks are made of. Nonbank financial service firms share similarities with nonfinancial firms offering services such as IT services in that inventory is insignificant as the service they provide requires human (or technology) interface with very little use of physical assets unlike the case in telecom or health care services. Receivables form the largest current assets in their balance sheets and fixed assets form a small proportion and play a supporting role unlike in manufacturing or even trading businesses.

But the similarity ends there. As we will see in some of the examples that follow, financial investments turn up as a strategic and significant operating asset and component of the business model in firms providing financial services. This is unlike goods-based and services firms discussed in previous chapters where financial investments played a more residual or strictly supporting role. Talking of bank and nonbank lending firms, the differences get starker as money becomes the hero of the story rather than playing a facilitator role.

Financial services offer a broad platter in which many unique business models exist. Almost all financial services perform the crucial function of financial intermediation in an economy. Put simply, financial intermedia-tion takes the shape of brokering deals or asset transformation and risk transfer. The former involves bringing together parties that have surplus funds and are looking for investment opportunities and those that have investment opportunities and are seeking funds for them. An example of asset transformation is transforming short-term assets such as deposits held by individuals into long-term assets such as housing loans held by the banks. Assets can be transformed across tenure, currency, or even risk-iness. Insurance firms engage in transfer of and reduction of risk across a system. Then there are financial services that conduct financial interme-diation of a very different kind, for example, rating firms. These enable banks and insurance firms in conducting their business by providing and disseminating much needed information about the different participants at very low cost to the system. Banks are very different from insurance companies, which are in turn very different from asset management firms. Within banks, the business model of commercial banks is quite different from that of investment banks. Within insurance, financial statements of life insurance are significantly different from that of nonlife insurance businesses.

This chapter will attempt to cover a few common business models that can form the overall schema for businesses that are offshoots of such primary business models. Financial statements of a commercial bank, a general insurance firm and a life insurance firm should give the reader a good first-level grip on what financial services are all about.

Analysis of the Financial Statements of a Commercial Bank

A commercial bank receives deposits from savers and lends to borrow-ers. The gross profit margin of the bank is simply the interest differential between what it charges borrowers and what it pays the savers. Besides this core business activity, a commercial bank provides various services on which it receives fees and commission. And besides the interest expense on deposits, the bank also incurs operating expenses just like any other firm on salaries, infrastructure, and running operations. This makes the business model of a bank sound extremely simple. But in reality, banks and financial services are one of the most complex businesses to manage. Let us understand this using the financial statements of ICICI Bank Ltd[1].

ICICI Bank is India's largest private sector bank and offers a comprehensive range of products and services through both offline and online channels. Besides commercial banking, ICICI Ltd. has subsidiaries engaged in investment banking, insurance as well as asset management. For the purpose of illustrating commercial banking business through financial statements, only standalone financial statements of ICICI Ltd., the commercial bank, have been taken. What is the difference between standalone and consolidated financial statements? While the former pertain to only the commercial banking business.—consolidated financial statements include the claim of the holding company (ICICI Bank) in all its subsidiaries depending on the stake it holds in the latter. Table 5.1 provides the standalone balance sheets of ICICI Bank for five consecutive years.

What are the striking differences between a bank's balance sheet and those which we have encountered thus far? First, the balance sheet does not seem to have classified assets and liabilities into current and noncurrent ones. Are all its assets and liabilities current or noncurrent? Or is it that liquidity is not a concern for banks? In fact, liquidity is of more concern to banks than probably most other businesses. And not all its assets or liabilities are of one or the other type. Banks too have a blend of both. Within deposits and borrowings on the liabilities side and within investments and advances on the assets side, there are items that are short term and others that have a longer tenure. Despite this, there is no restriction on long-term deposits (time deposits) being called on prematurely by depositors or for long-term advances to be paid off prematurely by borrowers. Similarly, a bank may sell off a long-term investment (held-to-maturity or HTM investment) or pay off a long-term borrowing prematurely.[2] This uncertainty coupled with the fact that most deposits are of short-term nature, while advances are of long-term nature, makes asset-liability management one of the most important functions of a bank and the related risk a major risk to manage.

---

[1]Source for ICICI Bank Ltd.'s financial statements: Annual reports of ICICI Bank Ltd. from https://www.icicibank.com/aboutus/investor-corner.page?
[2]Regulatory restrictions are placed on banks to trade HTM investments. Similarly, banks typically have penalties in place for premature withdrawal of deposits and premature loan repayment by customers.

Table 5.1 Balance sheets for ICICI Bank Ltd.

	As on				
	March 31, 2017	March 31, 2016	March 31, 2015	March 31, 2014	March 31, 2013
Sources of funds					
Share capital	11.71	11.70	11.67	11.62	11.58
Total reserves	987.80	885.66	792.62	720.52	655.48
Shareholder equity	999.51	897.36	804.29	732.13	667.06
Deposits	4,900.39	4,214.26	3,615.63	3,319.14	2,926.14
Borrowings	1,475.56	1,748.07	1,724.17	1,547.59	1,453.41
Other liab. and provisions	342.45	347.26	317.20	347.56	321.34
Total liabilities	**7,717.91**	**7,206.95**	**6,461.29**	**5,946.42**	**5,367.95**
Application of funds					
Cash and balance with RBI	317.02	271.06	256.53	218.22	190.53
Balances with banks and money at call and short notice	440.11	327.63	166.52	197.08	223.65
Investments	1,615.07	1,604.12	1,581.29	1,770.22	1,713.94
Advances	4,642.32	4,352.64	3,875.22	3,387.03	2,902.49
Net block	78.05	75.77	47.26	46.78	46.47
Other assets	625.35	575.74	534.48	327.09	290.87
Total assets	**7,717.91**	**7,206.95**	**6,461.29**	**5,946.42**	**5,367.95**
Contingent liability	10,309.94	9007.99	8519.78	7814.30	7899.89

Note: All amounts in INR billion.

Second, deposits are the dominant item on the liabilities side of the balance sheet. As part of debt funding, this puts the debt-to-equity ratio or financial leverage of ICICI Bank at a whopping 6.72× for FY2017 and marginally above 7× for all prior years. This is a magnitude of financial leverage we have not encountered so far. Is this normal for a bank or is ICICI Bank taking on too much risk? This is one of the most important and significant features of banks that puts them on a very different plane during financial and risk analysis. A debt–equity ratio of 7× is actually on the lower side when compared to the average Indian bank. High debt–equity ratio is woven into the basic business model of financial intermediation by commercial banks and the credit creation function of banks. Put simply, a bank that is started with INR 10 of equity capital may borrow INR 90, of which it keeps say INR 15 as cash reserves for liquidity purposes and lends INR 85 (INR 75 of deposits and INR 10 of equity) further to earn interest income. This INR 85 further creates a cycle of credit in the economy via the "credit multiplier." An initial deposit of INR 90 and equity investment of INR 10 has now created an additional deposit of INR 85 with no increase in money supply in the economy! So did we just create money out of thin air? Pretty much!

What if the people who gave the bank INR 90 came to the bank asking for their money? The bank has only INR 15 in hand! The business of banking is based on the premise that all depositors will never come to the bank at the same time to pull out all their money and INR 15 will be sufficient to take care of withdrawal requirements. The reader can now see why banking is an extremely risky business. The depositor will let her money remain with the bank and withdraw only what she needs if and only if she is convinced that her money with the bank is safe. This makes it imperative for banks to not only manage this humongous risk smartly but to also always maintain depositors' trust in them about the safety of the latter's money. If not, all the depositors will come asking for their INR 90 at the same time creating *a run on the bank*. The banking business model is not built to handle this situation and will necessarily collapse.

The third most important observation is on the assets side. Net block or fixed assets form a very tiny portion of total assets and advances are clearly the dominant item followed by investments. The reader will immediately realize how important it is that the banks lend depositors' money to the right parties so that it comes back safely and on time along with interest due on it. Credit risk therefore, becomes paramount in the business of banking. While other businesses sell their products and services to customers on credit and hence, also take on credit risk, there are three primary differences. First, for other businesses, offering credit to customers is a choice and not a compulsion (market competition might make it compulsory but the business model is not necessarily built as such) and second, the proportion of credit sales to total sales is likely to be quite low. On the contrary, in the case of the banking business, credit is what the business model is built on—it is not a choice. The third difference is that even if the firm offers credit to all its customers, for example, a motor vehicle manufacturer sells all his cars to his dealers on credit, the credit period normally spans a few days to a few months. For a bank, the period of credit can range from a few months to many years depending on the type of loan being extended.

In a nutshell, the primary source of funds for a commercial bank is its deposits; borrowings may or may not form a significant source and equity, interestingly, acts more as a security cover for the depositors/lenders rather than as a significant source of finance. The primary use of the funds is to deploy them in lending activities and on a smaller scale, investing them in financial assets. This automatically implies that commercial banking business rests on the margin a bank earns between its lending/investing and borrowing activities. This can be understood better from the bank's P&L statement (Table 5.2).

The difference between interest earned and interest expended is termed net interest income and it forms (should form) the largest component of a commercial bank's income. Other income comprises fees and commissions on services such as transaction support, loan proposal processing, card business, risk management services, etc. as well as capital gains/losses on sale of investments. Another important component of other income is the profit or loss from revaluation of investments. While this item may not be large in quantum for most periods in time, it is an inherent dynamic of a bank's investment portfolio. Investments that are not held to maturity need to be marked to market (MtM), which means they need to be expressed at their market values (as against book values for HTM investments, as HTM investments are expected to be

Table 5.2 Profit and loss statement for ICICI Bank Ltd.

	For year ended on day of				
	March 31, 2017	**March 31, 2016**	**March 31, 2015**	**March 31, 2014**	**March 31, 2013**
Income					
Interest earned	541.56	527.39	490.91	441.78	400.76
Interest expended	324.19	315.15	300.52	277.03	262.09
Net interest income	217.37	212.24	190.40	164.76	138.66
Other income	195.04	153.23	121.76	104.28	83.46
Total income	412.42	365.47	312.16	269.03	222.12
Expenditure					
Operating expenses	139.97	119.85	108.37	97.33	85.23
Cash operating profit	272.44	245.62	203.79	171.71	136.89
Depreciation	7.58	6.99	6.59	5.76	4.90
Provisions and contingencies	152.08	116.68	39.05	26.31	18.10
Profit before tax	112.79	121.96	158.15	139.63	113.90
Provision for tax	14.78	24.69	46.40	41.53	30.64
Profits after tax	**98.01**	**97.26**	**111.75**	**98.10**	**83.25**

Note: All amounts in INR billion.

redeemed at maturity values and fluctuations in their value do not affect the bank's financial position) in the balance sheet. As per Indian accounting rules, any notional loss on such revaluation has to be recognized in the P&L statement immediately, while any notional gain is accounted for in "Other comprehensive income" directly going into the reserves in the balance sheet. Rules in some other countries require both losses and gains to be recognized in the P&L statement similarly. What is important to understand is that despite these differences, the common understanding that investments are a core ingredient of banking and potential gains and losses on them need to be accounted for and get reflected in financial statements for prospective investors and decision makers to take calls based on these numbers. These numbers become significant during times of large interest rate swings and during economic instability.

Banks in India had been piling up longer-tenure debt securities as part of their investments portfolio in anticipation of interest rate cuts by the Reserve Bank of India (RBI) in the months to come. However, the yield on the government securities saw an unexpected upward movement during the last quarter of the calendar year 2017, and into the New Year. Banks therefore, had to take on huge MtM losses on their books on account of these investments that were unhedged.[3] These losses will show up in their third quarter results for FY2018 and possibly in their FY2018 annual results.

Other income also includes gain or loss on foreign exchange transactions and on sale of fixed assets. The P&L statement has only two line items for expenses before taxes—operating expenses and provisions and contingencies—the latter having overtaken the former as the larger component in the last 2 years. Clearly, operating expenses are of a cash nature, while provisions are of a noncash nature. Banking being (still) a human resources intensive business, employee-related expenses dominate operating expenses.

Having understood a bank's balance sheet at first brush, how does one analyze it? Can the DuPont framework work for a bank? The 4-way DuPont framework that was applied to all firms analyzed thus far is,

$$ROE = RES \times NOPAT \times ATR \times LEV, \text{ or}$$

$$ROE = [1 - Int/EBIT] \times [EBIT(1 - t)/Revenues] \times [Revenues/Assets] \times [Assets/Equity]$$

Can this framework be applied in a similar manner to ICICI Bank? If not, which part of the framework makes it difficult or not possible to do so? It helps to recollect what the above version of the DuPont framework essentially articulates. It helps to separate the operating performance of a firm from the effect of financial leverage. ROE is nothing but return

---

[3]While hedging protects against unanticipated interest rates movements, it also caps benefits from favorable interest rate movements. Banks were so certain of interest rate cuts that they were caught unawares by an upward sloping yield curve.

from operations (ROA) amplified by the equity multiplier resulting from financial leverage. And the line dividing operations from financing activities so far has been debt in the capital structure resulting in interest liability. Hence, (almost) all expenses other than interest expenses (and other incomes) were included in operations.

Why is this definition of operations problematic in case of banks? When debt (deposits) becomes the primary source for a business' operating asset, which is cash and the interest on such debt becomes the primary operating expense, interest can no longer be treated exclusively as a finance cost. In other words, unlike nonbank firms, interest expense becomes an operating expense and EBIT (and NOPAT) ceases to be a meaningful concept. Hence, the original 3-way version of the DuPont framework becomes a better analytical tool for banks:

$$ROE = \text{Net Profit Margin (NPM)} \times ATR \times LEV$$

In other words, NPM cannot be broken down into operating profit margin and impact of financing costs easily. Does this mean that all interest expenses of a bank are of operating nature? A more basic question to ask is how one should decide which portion of the debt is for operations and which portion for financing purposes. Or to put it differently, which uses of funds can be classified as operating and which ones as financing? This does not have a straightforward answer and one approach could be to classify all lending and investments in financial assets as operating activities and all investment in fixed assets as investment activities. This is not completely correct as very often banks park their surplus funds with the central bank or in other investments akin to nonfinancial firms. These are better classified as investments than operations. Second, as can be seen from the balance sheet of ICICI Bank, fixed assets form an insignificant part of a bank's use of funds. Hence, by this classification, investment activities of a bank too become insignificant and practically all funding can be seen to be used for operations. The reader will get a better view of this in the cash flow statement. But for now, it is clear that separating out the interest expense into operating and financing expenses is not only difficult, it might be a meaningless exercise. Hence, a three-way DuPont analysis works better for banks (and other lending businesses) as shown in Table 5.3.

Table 5.3 DuPont analysis for ICICI Bank Ltd.

	For year ended on day of			
	March 31, 2017	March 31, 2016	March 31, 2015	March 31, 2014
Net Profit Margin (NPM)	23.77%	26.61%	35.80%	36.47%
Asset Turnover Ratio (ATR)	0.055	0.054	0.050	0.048
Financial Leverage (LEV)	7.87	8.03	8.08	8.09
Return on Assets (ROA)	1.31%	1.42%	1.80%	1.73%
Return on Equity (ROE)	10.33%	11.43%	14.55%	14.02%

Besides the fact that profit margins are measured at a net profit level after interest expenses, how does the output of the DuPont analysis for a bank differ from firms that have been studied so far? As already discussed earlier, LEV is significantly higher than the most levered firm seen in the previous chapters. Also, ATR is extremely low as compared to ATR of manufacturing/trading as well as service firms. The ROA almost completely rests on the NPM and the ROE is almost completely driven by LEV. In Chapter 2, while discussing the DuPont framework, it was averred that a firm whose ROE is primarily driven by LEV rather than its ROA is operating a very risky business model and this may not be sustainable especially during downturns when operations might come under strain.

For a bank, however, this is part of its design and business model as already discussed. Financial leverage is not a choice for a commercial bank and it cannot operate on leverage as low as is found in nonfinancial service firms[4]. An ROA at 2 percent is not bad at all in this industry. In fact, it is not possible to raise this ROA by much from here. Why is that so?

---

[4]Miller (1995) refutes this argument that banks necessarily have to be highly levered. He says that a bank can choose to fund its loans and investments largely by equity as well. While this in itself is not incorrect, it takes away from the basic function of banks as financial intermediaries that help create credit in an economy by tapping into household savings.

Clearly, ICICI Bank seems to be performing quite well on the margins front. So any casual observer is bound to think that any improvement is possible only on the ATR front. And she will not be wrong. However, to what extent can ATR be improved over current levels? Before we start discussing this point, provided in Table 5.4 is another version of ICICI Bank's DuPont analysis. What is the difference between the two sets of numbers?

ROA and ROE are the same as earlier; naturally, LEV is also the same as earlier. The difference is in the components of ROA—NPM and ATR are now different. NPM has reduced by over 10 percentage points for each of the years and ATR has increased by between 4 and 5 percentage points for all the years. The percentage increase in ATR is exactly matched by the percentage decrease in NPM, leaving ROA unchanged. Table 5.3 had used net interest income plus other income to compute revenues in its calculation of NPM and ATR, while Table 5.4 has used gross interest income plus other income as proxy for revenues to calculate the same ratios. Neither versions can be called correct or incorrect so long as the analyst is aware of the inputs and maintains consistency across time periods and banks when comparing.

The second version in Table 5.4 is however, more in line with the DuPont analysis that has been conducted for firms in Chapters 3 and 4. The essence of profit margin is to decipher the profits (operating or net)

Table 5.4 DuPont analysis for ICICI Bank Ltd. on gross revenues basis

	For year ended on day of			
	March 31, 2017	March 31, 2016	March 31, 2015	March 31, 2014
Net Profit Margin (NPM)	13.31%	14.29%	18.24%	17.97%
Asset Turnover Ratio (ATR)	9.87%	9.96%	9.88%	9.65%
Financial Leverage (LEV)	7.87	8.03	8.08	8.09
Return on Assets (ROA)	1.31%	1.42%	1.80%	1.73%
Return on Equity (ROE)	10.33%	11.43%	14.55%	14.02%

that a firm manages to earn out of the gross revenues that it makes by selling goods or services to clients. In that sense, gross interest earned is a better reflection of the top-line for a bank. Similarly, the essence of ATR is to understand how well a firm's assets have been utilized to generate top-line revenues. A commercial bank uses loans and advances as well as investments in financial assets to generate interest income. Hence, gross interest income better reflects the rate of utilization of a bank's financial assets and as will be seen further, makes for better analyses.

Drivers of a Commercial Bank's Profit Margins

With the numbers laid out in Table 5.4, the net profit margins do not seem as impressive any more but they are not bad either. What is probably worrying is that they have been trending downwards. Using the principle of largest first, compute the proportion of the interest earned that is going into paying interest on deposits and borrowings. This has actually reduced significantly over the 5 years from over 65 percent to less than 60 percent, leaving a margin of more than 40 percent for other expenses and profits. This calculation alone would have given the reader a good idea of the importance of managing interest rates on deployment of funds (advances and investments) and interest rates on sources of funds (deposits and borrowings). The difference between the two *rates of interest* is termed the bank's **spread**. A bank has varying buckets and types of advances lent at varying rates of interest and similarly, deposits and borrowings of various tenures and terms that attract different interest rates. In order to compute the spread, an average interest income rate and an average interest expense rate is used.

Spread = [Total interest income/Average interest-bearing assets] −
[Total interest expenses/Average interest-bearing liabilities]

OR, Spread = Yield on interest-bearing assets − Cost of
interest-bearing liabilities

Interest-bearing assets comprise largely loans and advances as well as financial investments that yield interest income. Interest-bearing liabilities are typically those deposits on which interest is payable (current deposits do not attract interest) and borrowings. The spread is a crucial decision variable in the hands of a bank's management that sets the base for the bank's profit margin on its core activity.

Operating expenses have increased, albeit marginally, over the 5 years. The cost-to-income ratio, which is measured as operating expenses divided by total income, including noninterest income, works out to either a reasonable 17 percent to 19 percent or a much higher 32 percent to 39 percent range, depending on how revenue is measured. For the sake of consistency, let us take the former set of numbers. The increase in operating expenses is not large enough to explain the more than 5 percentage point dip in net margins. In fact, at this stage, the cash operating profit margin (on gross interest income) for ICICI Bank has grown impressively from 28 percent in FY2013 to nearly 39 percent in FY2017. Besides depreciation, which is quite insignificant in proportion, the only other expense item is *Provisions and Contingencies*. This expense item has ballooned in FY2016 and FY2017, thereby explaining the sharp dip in margins from FY2015 to FY2016. What are these provisions for and what has caused them to shoot up so?

When a firm sells goods (or services) on credit to its customers or lends to its customers and suppliers, it exposes itself to credit risk—the possibility that the customer/borrower may default partially or fully. Conservatism demands that the lender *provide for* such a contingency. How is such a provision made? Just like a household keeps aside some funds from its current income for contingencies such as medical emergencies, a firm makes a provision out of its current revenues for such a possibility of default. Unlike a household it does not set aside physical cash (even a household need not set aside physical cash but may make a charge against current income so as to reduce the amount of disposable income it has) but the charge against revenues reduces the distributable profits that the firm has at the end of the period. This automatically forces the firm to cut down on dividends or other investments and signals to the market the embedded risk in the firm's financials.

The entire business of lending of commercial banks revolves around exposing itself to credit risk and hence, making provisions for such contingencies becomes a core activity. It takes a far bigger shape and scale in banking than it does in nonfinance businesses where substantial sales may be in cash. Having established that such provisions need to be created, how does one decide on the percentage or quantum of provisioning? Commonsense says that it should be based on the management's perception of the probability and quantum of default and slight overprovisioning is always better than underprovisioning. Overprovisioning means that the amount of provisions accumulated over the years is greater than the amount of defaults that are likely to happen. Taking the analogy of a household again, the family would want its contingency fund to be more than sufficient for any medical emergency that it may be faced with, with something left over. This philosophy and practice works quite well for most goods-based and nonfinancial services firms unless they are facing a dire situation in the market. However, in the case of banks it is not possible to have an overprovisioned scenario simply due to the scale of the activity and peculiarity of its business model as we will see further.

The RBI, India's central bank, mandated that banks should try to achieve a total **provisioning coverage ratio (PCR)** of 70 percent. PCR is calculated as total provisions divided by nonperforming assets, that is, assets that have shown some default and hence, classified as nonperforming. This clearly shows that overprovisioning has neither been the mandate nor may be practical in the business of commercial banking. However, such underprovisioning works fine on two conditions. First, that the nonperforming assets (NPA) are clearly identified and revealed in the books, and second, all NPA do not liquidate themselves at the same time. Loans and advances by banks that have interest and principal overdue for 90 days are termed NPA.

With this background in place, one can try to understand what happened during FY2016 in the Indian banking system to warrant a spike in provisions. Most banks had flouted rule number one as mentioned in the last paragraph. Recognition of NPA was not done in a transparent manner over some of the previous years and bad news had been brushed under the carpet. Under directive from the RBI all banks had to come out clean and reveal the true scale of NPA they had in their books. Consequently, the existing provisions fell drastically short of requirements and again the RBI intervened and forced banks to beef up their provisions. Banks were, thus, forced to charge this entire deficit in provisioning to the current year's revenues. As a result, many banks posted net losses for the first time in their history. For perspective, even after the huge provisioning undertaken by ICICI Bank in FY2016 and FY2017, their PCR stood at just a shade over 40 percent! The reader will now be able to see the previous years' as well as the last 2 years' performance metrics in a new light. The numbers cannot likely be taken at face value.

We will return to NPA and provisioning when understanding loans and advances more closely.

Drivers of a Commercial Bank's Asset Productivity

The next important parameter of the DuPont framework is ATR, which measures how well the assets of a bank are being utilized to generate revenues. Prima facie, the ATR posted for ICICI Bank looks very poor. The figures indicate that the bank is barely able to squeeze out revenues equivalent of 10 percent of the value of assets it has been deploying. Compare this to the other firms that have been analyzed in the previous chapters. HUL posted ATR upwards of 300 percent each year and TCS' numbers were anywhere from 160 percent to over 200 percent. BAL was a relatively poor performer at ATR between 45 percent and 60 percent; even Bhushan Steel that has been pushed to bankruptcy was performing at over 20 percent ATR. So might concluding inefficiency in asset utilization by ICICI Bank be a correct inference?

The largest asset component in a commercial bank's balance sheet is Loans and Advances and the second largest is Investments. At north of 80 percent, it is a no-brainer that the utilization rate of these two asset sets will drive the overall ATR of the bank. The revenue stream arising from both these asset groups is interest income (capital gains/losses on investments most often are smaller in quantum and tend to be more erratic). The interest income is a function of the quantum of assets deployed and the rates of interest at which they are deployed. Given that the risk-free rate of interest prevailing in the Indian market has been between 8 percent and 6 percent, applying even a 10 percent for risk premium on average will mean an interest rate of 16 percent to 18 percent on loans and advances. In other words, the ATR of the lending function of a bank is limited by the interest rate prevailing in the economy. Too high an ATR on this business will require the bank to take unwarranted risk on its credit portfolio.

Does this mean that commercial banking cannot see ATR greater than, say, 15 percent on average? Further, in a falling interest rate scenario ATRs would only contract, worsening returns. Consequently, the need for bank management to improve and maintain their profit margins becomes even more important. Banks world over have started paying more attention to nonfund-based business, that is, business that earns them fees, commissions, and the like—income that is classified under "Other Income." These businesses include facilitating trade by opening letters of credit, providing bank guarantees, cards business, and other value-add services. These and similar such services offer far greater economies of scale thereby, enabling greater utilization of investment per rupee or dollar. Of course, they require investment in fixed costs such as infrastructure, trained personnel, and marketing. If a bank gets its game right here, such nonfund businesses can help enhance asset utilization and consequently, returns on assets. Else it can backfire badly with investment in assets that the bank is either unable to leverage adequately for revenue or is generating revenues at high cost thereby, sacrificing margin.

The productivity of a commercial bank's largest component of assets—loans and advances—is measured by the **Net Interest Margin (NIM).** This is a very important performance metric for all financial services whose primary business is lending. NIM is measured as the net interest income divided by average interest-bearing assets. Readers should note that NIM includes all interest income and average interest-bearing assets include investments that earn interest income. So this is not purely a measure of a bank's lending activity but significantly so. Considering that the net interest income would make up for a significant portion of a bank's gross incomes and interest-bearing assets make up a substantial portion of its balance sheet, NIM is a key driver of a commercial bank's (or any lending institution's) ROA. ICICI Bank's NIM has ranged between 3.4 percent and 3.7 percent in the last 4 years taken for this case. The graph in Figure 5.1 shows the relationship between NIM and ROA of ICICI Bank for FY2014 through FY2017.

From March 2014 to March 2015, both NIM and ROA improved and from March 2016 to March 2017, both saw dips. However, the

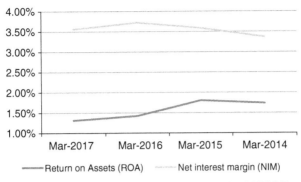

Figure 5.1 Correlation between NIM and ROA for ICICI Bank

intermediate year FY2016 ending on March 31, 2016, saw an increasing NIM but a perceptible drop in ROA. While NIM is a large contributor to the ROA, on the income side if a bank's Other Income is significant, the effect of NIM on ROA correspondingly diminishes. This does not seem to be the case at ICICI Bank as incomes from both sources—net interest income as well as other income—increased by similar quantum. ROA is influenced by expenses not forming part of NIM. In the case of ICICI Bank, similar to almost all Indian banks during the year, provisions and contingencies had to be increased disproportionately higher than an increase in net interest income, thereby more than negating the positive impact of a growing NIM on ROA.[5]

Information Within and Outside a Bank's Balance Sheet

A bank's balance sheet has a wealth of information that helps understand the bank's business strategy and helps explain its performance more completely. As already discussed earlier, the essence of commercial banking is taking deposits and making loans. This makes the deposits on the liabilities side and the loans/advances on the assets side the most important items on a commercial bank's balance sheet. Accordingly, the credit–deposit ratio or the CD ratio is a popularly used measure to gauge how

---

[5]This divergence cannot continue for long as bad loans will not earn interest and this will impact NIM as well. Past interest income recognized in a bank's P&L statement but not subsequently received will also have to be reversed.

active a bank is in the credit market. It also provides some indication of whether the deposits are deployed for credit or are being parked in lazy investments. It is also seen as a measure of the conservativeness or otherwise of a bank; a bank with low CD ratio may be seen as more conservative and risk-averse and this is bound to show up in its spreads, NIM, NPM, and ROA. Table 5.5 lays out some key ratios applicable to the banking industry, particularly commercial banks.

Contingent Liabilities are off-balance sheet items and, the reader would have noticed, are much larger for banks in relation to their balance sheet size than were for nonfinancial firms seen earlier. Unlike the nonfinancial firms where contingent liabilities typically comprise legal cases with clients or the tax authorities, for banks these include contracts entered into with clients—letters of credit or bank guarantees on behalf of clients, derivatives contracts, etc. Essentially, in the case of banks these arise from core business and are unavoidable unlike for the other firms where legal tangles can be avoidable. At more than 1,000 percent of net worth, clearly the exposure a bank has to potential loss should any of the guarantees get invoked or should any of the derivative contracts go against the bank (which is very much possible as many such contracts are zero-sum games) is huge, to say the least. It has the potential to wipe off the bank's net worth many times over, driving the institution into bankruptcy. A stakeholder, be it an investor, employee, or even a depositor (deposits up to a limit are insured in most countries) should be cognizant of this fact as this enhances the risk of insolvency for the bank.

This, coupled with high leverage ratio—which again is natural for a bank—makes a banking firm far more exposed to insolvency risk as compared to a nonfinancial firm. So how do banks counter this risk and provide assurance to stakeholders?

It is for precisely the above reasons that banks are much more regulated than are nonfinancial businesses.[6] Each country has their laws that govern the banks and their businesses. Indian banks are regulated by the RBI and governed by the Banking Regulation Act for public sector banks and the Companies Act for the ones in the private sector. Besides this, banks globally have adopted the Basel norms that bring about uniformity

---

[6]Nonfinancial businesses, such as telecom and airlines, are also highly regulated, albeit for different reasons.

Table 5.5 Key financial ratios for ICICI Bank Ltd.

	For year ended on day of				
	March 31, 2017	March 31, 2016	March 31, 2015	March 31, 2014	March 31, 2013
Credit–deposit ratio (CD ratio)	0.95	1.03	1.07	1.02	0.99
Investment–deposit ratio (ID ratio)	0.33	0.38	0.44	0.53	0.59
Gross nonperforming Assets (GNPA)%*	8.33%	5.68%	3.75%	3.01%	3.20%
Net nonperforming Assets (NNPA)%*	5.43%	2.98%	1.61%	0.97%	0.77%
Provisioning coverage ratio (PCR)	40.19%	50.56%	58.56%	68.61%	76.78%
Capital to risk-weighted assets (RWA) ratio (CRAR)*	17.39%	16.64%	17.02%	17.70%	18.74%
Leverage ratio (times)	6.72	7.03	7.03	7.12	7.05
Key performance ratios					
Net Interest Margin (NIM)	3.56%	3.72%	3.59%	3.37%	
Net Profit Margin (NPM)	13.31%	14.29%	18.24%	17.97%	17.19%
Return on Assets (ROA)	1.31%	1.42%	1.80%	1.73%	
Return on Equity (ROE)	10.33%	11.43%	14.55%	14.02%	
GNPA (in INR billion)*	421.59	262.21	150.95	105.06	96.08
NNPA (in INR billion)*	252.17	129.63	62.56	32.98	22.31
Contingent liability to net worth%*	1,031.50%	1003.84%	1,059.29%	1,067.33%	1,184.29%

*These ratios cannot be computed directly from the data appearing in the financial statements. The amounts of GNPA and NNPA have been taken from data published by the RBI.

in their functioning and approach to risk. The Basel norms are revised periodically with changing complexion of risk. Basel III, which came into being after the 2007 to 2008 global financial crisis is under adoption at various stages by banking systems across. Changes to Basel III (informally called Basel IV), primarily around risk-weighted assets, and the resulting impact on regulatory capital, were endorsed in December 2017.

The capital to risk-weighted assets ratio (CRAR), popularly known as the capital adequacy ratio is one of the key measures prescribed by the Basel rules. Simply put, CRAR is calculated as equity capital divided by risk-weighted assets (RWA). However, these inputs are not directly observable from the final balance sheets of a bank. Components of capital—Tier-I, Tier-II, etc.—as well as weights to be assigned to different types of assets—advances, investments, cash equivalents as well as others like fixed assets and for different types of risks such as credit, market, and operational risks—are detailed out in the rules. A weighted average thus computed gives the RWA figure. The Basel-III rules require banks to have a CRAR of at least 11.5 percent including capital conservation buffer. As can be seen from Table 5.6, ICICI Bank is in a very comfortable position from this point of view. Readers should notice how 11.5 percent compares with the equity-to-assets ratio one might see for nonfinancial firms.

Table 5.6 Equity to total assets ratios across industries

	For year ended on day of				
	March 31, 2017	March 31, 2016	March 31, 2015	March 31, 2014	March 31, 2013
Banking (ICICI Bank)	17.39%	16.64%	17.02%	17.70%	18.74%
IT Services (TCS Ltd.)	84.42%	80.69%	70.60%	74.67%	66.31%
Retail (HUL)	43.08%	44.57%	28.08%	25.88%	23.86%
Infrastructure (Bhushan)	(2.62)%	3.83%	15.39%	18.49%	22.04%
Telecom (BAL)	32.07%	32.16%	23.56%	35.24%	34.44%

Note: For all other industries/firms, a simple shareholder funds to total assets has been used. Corresponding ratio for ICICI Bank works out to between 12 percent and 13 percent for all the years.

The next lowest equity/total assets ratio is for Bhushan and BAL—the first that is facing bankruptcy proceedings and the second that is holding more than optimal debt in its balance sheet. Even these two firms had much higher "capital adequacy" in the initial 2 years. HUL started out with an equity ratio around the same as Bhushan's but had nearly doubled it by FY2017 end. TCS' equity ratio clearly indicates the high safety net an asset-light service firm can afford. While each of the above firms may not be the best representatives of their respective industries, the numbers clearly indicate the equity net a manufacturing firm can afford as against a retail firm. At a next level, the equity net a goods-based firm can afford versus a nonfinancial service firm is also very evident. The numbers clearly bring out how a banking firm's service model is different from other asset-light service firms' and how therefore, while the latter like TCS can work with negligible or even zero debt and build huge equity base, a bank is limited by its business model forcing it to carry much higher debt. This also shows the narrow margin of error a bank enjoys vis-à-vis other businesses before it can slip into insolvency.

To take a simple example, say a bank holds INR 100 of assets that are supported by INR 90 of deposits and the rest by equity. The bank lends INR 90 to various borrowers and of this, INR 20 turns distressed.[7] If the bank manages to recover anything less than INR 10 out of this distressed loan, it would have eroded its entire equity and would be insolvent. While this is a simplistic scenario, this gives a good indication of how the 11.5 percent minimum CRAR may fall inadequate or may not suffice to make bank insolvencies very improbable. Hence, banks require other safeguards for their investors, especially depositors so that they continue to keep their hard-earned money with banks. The deposit insurance scheme that is in place in all countries with varying limits and rules is meant to provide one such layer of safety.

Having discussed the need for capital adequacy, the logical next step is to understand how the extent of loan losses is measured. The GNPA and NNPA ratios in Table 5.5 provide this information. While recognition

---

[7]The reader should realize that this assumption implies a gross NPA ratio of 22 percent, which is very high. But it is high rates of bad loans that push a bank into insolvency. This highlights the importance of credit risk management in banks.

of an asset as NPA is defined by the banking laws of the land, in India 90 days of default puts an asset in this category. The GNPA ratio is simply the amount of gross NPAs as on the date to total advances on that date. From 3.20 percent of gross advances in FY2013, ICICI Bank has seen more than 8 percent[8] of its gross advances turn bad by the end of FY2017. Readers will recollect the discussion on provisions for bad loans earlier in the chapter. The PCR is the extent to which provisions have been built to cushion the impact of bad loans. Clearly, ICICI Bank's cushion or provision has not kept pace with the build-up of bad loans. While in absolute terms provisions have increased, they came down from 77 percent in FY2013 to cover only 40 percent of gross NPAs by the end of FY2017.

The unprovided-for portion of the gross NPAs constitutes the net NPAs (NNPA). The reader will recollect that while nonfinancial businesses typically might overprovide for their bad loans, which means they will have no NNPA (negative technically), banks are more likely to underprovide. Why is this so? Let us take the example of ICICI Bank for FY2017. During FY2017, the bank created provisions of INR 152 billion. The NNPA figure of INR 252 billion indicates the unprovided-for NPAs as at the end of the year. Had the bank provided for these as well, it would have posted a loss of INR 140 billion before taxes! To put this in perspective, the GNPA ratio of the bank at the end of FY2017 was only 8.33 percent, which is not a very large percentage of gross credit sales in most nonfinancial businesses.

We have already discussed the limit to the ATR that the business of lending affords a bank. Taking our simple illustration further, total loans of INR 90 will translate into gross revenues of say, INR 13.50 even if an ATR of 15 percent is assumed. Applying a healthy margin of 40 percent of cash operating profits yields a profit figure of INR 5.40. This works to only 6 percent of its total advances. In other words, if the bank were to have a PCR of 100 percent, it cannot afford a GNPA ratio of above

---

[8]While the rules for recognizing NPA seem simple, in reality it is quite complex with consortium and group lending on the one hand, and lending to parent and subsidiary companies on the other. As a result, for many banks there have been differences between NPA declared by the bank and as computed by the RBI. The data for ICICI Bank presented here are as per the bank's declaration.

6 percent without booking operating losses. To be fair, this is not a tall order if the economic climate is healthy and the bank has tight credit risk assessment and monitoring systems in place. But insolvencies normally do not happen during the upswing of an economic cycle. Credits that were genuinely good during the upswings can turn bad during downswings. Bhushan Steel is a case in point. It is in these situations that banks see high GNPA and NNPA ratios and naturally low PCR. This is evident from the trajectory of these three ratios for ICICI Bank itself.

Having discussed nonperforming assets and the protective shield offered to depositors around them, we turn our attention to the source of these bad assets. The source is loans and investments—the core business of a bank! The CD ratio indicates that ICICI Bank has been lending out close to or more than 100 percent worth of its deposits. It is only in FY2017 that this ratio dipped to 95 percent—a year when credit off-take was poor across the Indian economy owing to the twin problems caused by the NPA crisis and the sudden demonetization of two currency denominations.[9] Banks do not lend only out of deposits collected; they can finance lending activities through borrowings and equity capital. Therefore, even after providing for statutory reserves as mandated by the central bank, the total lending by a bank can be close to or even more than 100 percent of the bank's deposits. Clearly, for a bank posting such high CD ratio borrowings and equity capital would form a reasonable proportion of total sources of funds on its balance sheet. For perspective, government-owned banks in India on average, posted CD ratio of less than 70 percent as against almost 87 percent on average by private sector banks for the year FY2017.[10]

Banks are mandated to park some portion of their deposits with the central bank in the form of government bonds and other approved

---

[9]The demonetization of INR 500 and INR 1,000 in November 2016 led to huge cash inflows into banks' coffers, spiking up short-term liquidity. Simultaneously, the uncertain environment coupled with the NPA crisis made banks cautious about lending, leading to a drop in credit and rise in unutilized deposits.

[10]Sourced from the table titled "Bank Group-wise Select Ratios of Scheduled Commercial Banks" in the Statistical Tables Relating to Banks in India published by the Reserve Bank of India on its official website.

forms. This is another method by which the regulator ensures buffer and safety for deposits. Over and above the mandated minimum, banks hold investments in certain approved securities as well as in other securities such as bonds and equity. These could be strategic, that is, held with a view to earn interest income or dividends and capital gains or these could be temporary parking avenues of excess cash. Investments normally are not planned to provide returns as are advances. Therefore, high ID ratios may not be taken very kindly by the stock market. ICICI Bank's ID ratio has consistently followed a downward trajectory from a very high 60 percent in FY2013 to 33 percent in FY2017. Prima facie it might appear ICICI Bank has excessive slack on its liabilities side, which it possibly may have been holding in the initial years, but such high ID ratios are also a function of deposits constituting 55 percent of its total liabilities in FY2013 that increased to 63 percent by FY2017. This is in contrast to the government-owned banks that also posted similar ID ratio of over 30 percent in the last 2 years but with a deposit ratio of over 80 percent. Why is credit and investments by banks measured against deposits?

Deposits are meant to be the largest and a nondiscretionary source of funds for any commercial bank. And deposits involve a cost. Therefore, it is imperative for a bank to monitor how these deposits are deployed. Banking has become a commodity business and spreads enjoyed by banks have narrowed over the years, especially in developed markets. In such a scenario, banks have to be very careful with balancing the quantum of funds raised—whether through deposits or through borrowings—and deployment of these funds. If high ID ratio is primarily reflective of a bank parking its excess funds either due to lack of credit opportunities or simply conservatism, it directly hits the bank's spreads and margins and hence, ROA. Even if the investments have not resulted from mere parking of excess funds, earning on investments is not a bank's core business. Besides lending, banks have diversified into nonfund businesses, as described earlier, that afford it greater scale economies and margins. Hence, over time, the definition of what is core for a bank has also been undergoing change.

We have already discussed the performance ratios earlier. However, juxtaposing them against one another and looking at them comprehensively as in Table 5.5 provides an interesting picture. As for any bank, NIMs for ICICI Bank are in single digits, while the NPMs are far higher. This is attributed to two factors. First, NIM is calculated on a bank's earning assets base, while NPM is calculated on its revenues base. Revenues are far lower than the assets a bank possesses, thanks to low ATR possible in the industry. Second, NIM includes only interest income and expenses, while NPM includes other income and expenses too. For a bank that earns significant noninterest income and enjoys scale economies, NPM will be much higher than what its interest-based business earns.

Going further, ROA, which is a comprehensive measure of performance of all operations of the bank is a very low figure. As already discussed, this is the impact of a very low ATR on reasonably high NPM. An ATR of close to 10 percent coupled with a healthy margin of say, 20 percent translates to 2 percent ROA. The next and final step in the ladder is the ROE, which again is a high figure. The low ATR is amplified by the very high leverage employed by a bank that takes ROE to a level *that the market finds acceptable.*

Cash Flow Statements of a Commercial Bank

For a business where the line between operating and financing activities, and sometimes between operating and investment activities, is blurred, it is interesting to see how the cash flow statement might distinguish between them and the insights that can be gleaned therefrom.

Let us begin by enumerating the main differences between the cash flow statement (CFS) of a bank as in Table 5.7 and a nonfinancial services firm.

1. Unlike the latter, in a bank's CFS the adjustment for nonoperating items, when arriving at cash flow from operations (CFO), does not include adding back interest expenses and subtracting interest income from the profit before tax. Interest income and expenses are operating items for banks.

2. Since interest income is an operating income for banks, the assets generating interest income, namely advances and investments, are operating assets unlike in nonfinancial firms where they are investment

Table 5.7 Cash flow statements for ICICI Bank Ltd.

	For year ended on day of				
	March 31, 2017	March 31, 2016	March 31, 2015	March 31, 2014	March 31, 2013
Profit before taxes	112.79	121.96	158.20	139.68	113.97
Adjustments for expenses and provisions	75.48	73.36	27.41	17.18	17.37
(Increase)/ decrease in investments	0.33	67.19	47.16	78.31	(22.72)
(Increase)/ decrease in advances	(475.01)	(568.48)	(539.60)	(510.44)	(380.24)
Increase/ (decrease) in deposits	686.13	598.63	296.49	393.00	371.14
(Increase)/ decrease in other assets	(17.19)	(10.78)	17.50	(50.81)	12.99
Increase/ (decrease) in other liab. and prov.	56.68	(1.79)	(13.72)	21.38	30.50
Refund/ (payment) of direct taxes	(46.97)	(55.79)	(41.68)	(41.61)	(31.99)
Cash flow from operating activities	**392.23**	**224.28**	**(48.24)**	**46.69**	**111.02**
Investments in subsidiaries and/or JVs	58.78	41.46	8.72	6.13	4.05
Income from subsidiaries JVs/associates	14.19	15.38	15.75	13.16	9.42
Purchase of fixed assets	(7.83)	(7.00)	(7.87)	(6.78)	(5.88)
Proceeds from sale of fixed assets	0.12	0.65	0.31	1.99	1.24

Table 5.7 (*continued*)

	For year ended on day of				
	March 31, 2017	March 31, 2016	March 31, 2015	March 31, 2014	March 31, 2013
(Purchase)/ sale of HTM securities	5.20	(89.98)	(108.91)	(136.96)	(103.14)
Cash flow from investing activities	**70.45**	**(39.50)**	**(92.00)**	**(122.46)**	**(94.32)**
Proceeds from issue of share capital	1.77	2.82	3.48	0.76	0.45
Proceeds from long-term borrowings	312.18	332.68	352.03	269.60	50.68
Repayment of long-term borrowings	(411.33)	(261.95)	(217.59)	(163.84)	0.00
Net proceeds from short-term borrowings	(174.60)	(47.67)	41.04	(12.69)	0.00
Dividend and dividend tax paid	(31.81)	(31.74)	(28.91)	(25.45)	(21.23)
Cash flow from financing activities	**(303.79)**	**(5.85)**	**150.06**	**68.38**	**29.90**
Effect of exchange fluctuations	(0.45)	(3.29)	(2.07)	8.52	5.28
Net increase in cash and equivalents	**158.89**	**178.93**	**9.82**	**(7.40)**	**46.60**
Cash and cash equivalents at beginning	598.69	423.05	415.30	414.18	362.29
Cash and cash equivalents at end	757.13	598.69	423.05	415.30	414.18

Note: All figures are in INR billion; JV stands for joint ventures.

assets.[11] Increase and decrease in these items is therefore, adjusted for arriving at CFO. The exception is HTM securities that are investments made with a view to be held until maturity (as against parking temporary excess funds) and earn returns. Most often these investments are made in order to fulfill the statutory reserve requirements imposed on a bank. HTM securities are treated as investment items.

3. Since interest expense is an operating expense, the liabilities generating interest expense should be operating liabilities. Correspondingly, deposits held by banks are treated as operating liabilities and adjusted for in the computation of CFO. However, borrowings from the market are treated as financing activities. It is important to mention here that in America rules require banks to classify deposit-taking activity as financing activities. Academics and some practitioners (Mulford et al., 2009) have called out this practice saying that this makes the cash flow statement, and especially the CFO segment, meaningless.[12]

This treatment not only creates a dichotomy between classification of the liabilities vis-à-vis the classification of the corresponding interest expense but also presumes a certain role for monies received through deposits versus that received through borrowings.

By classifying all borrowings in financing activity, it is presumed that funds raised through market borrowings will never be lent in the ordinary course of business and will be only used to create other assets. This is not true as we have seen already, especially of many banks in the private sector that post CD ratios of close to 100 percent or more. Besides, even if this was a valid assumption and hence, treatment of borrowings, all interest expense on account of market borrowings should also ideally

---

[11]Even in nonfinancial firms, advances can be treated as operating assets when they arise in the normal course of operations of the firm rather than being a decision to invest excess cash. For example, advances to vendors, dealers, and even employees are often treated as operating assets.

[12]Besides classification of deposits as operating versus financial liabilities, investments are classified under CFO or CFI based on whether they are HTM or available for trading. Reclassification between these two categories can have implications for performance as CFO can change substantially without any change to overall cash position of the bank (Torfason, 2014).

form part of financing activities. Further, such interest expense should be separated from the interest expense on deposits when computing net interest income in the P&L statement and should appear as deduction from operating profits.

Because of lack of uniformity among banks about the utilization of market borrowings and the difficulty in making such segregation, industry practice has been to assume deposits to fund current assets and borrowings to fund investment activities. This assumption is fine so long as borrowings constitute a minor part of the balance sheet but can lead to incorrect decisions otherwise. However, some banks prefer to classify deposits and borrowings in operating activities, irrespective of the use the latter is put to.

This practice can also be defended on the ground that even in nonfinancial services firms, some part of the equity and debt funding goes into funding current assets (or should do so). In the same vein, a bank's equity capital and borrowings can be partly used for lending while still being classified as financing liabilities. The issue is only about the interest expense on such debt that is not separated out from interest expense on account of operations.

All in all, the CFS of a bank suffers from certain inherent issues arising from the business model that makes it not as useful a statement as it is for nonbanking firms. The CFS of a bank fails to provide significant incremental information over the P&L statement and balance sheet in its current form.

Understanding the Business of Insurance

A financial intermediary, an insurance company shares certain core similarities with a bank but differs in many major ways as well. While a commercial bank's essential raison d'etre is bringing together lenders and borrowers while transforming assets in the process, an insurer is a risk absorber and dissipater for individuals and economic constituents.

The essence of an insurance company's business is to take over the risk naturally arising to another party in exchange for a payment. The contractual arrangement binds the insurer to make good any loss the insured suffers, irrespective of the insurer's financial state. Therefore, it becomes imperative for the insurance company to run a more delicate trade-off between profitability, liquidity, and solvency than is the case for a nonfinancial services business. Even a commercial bank as we saw earlier, does a tightrope walk balancing these three imperatives.

Unlike all businesses that have been discussed thus far, including banks, insurance business is one where the customer—called policyholder—appears explicitly as a stakeholder in the financial statements. All businesses discussed earlier had only the lenders' interests appearing separate from other suppliers and stakeholders, apart from of course, the shareholder. In the insurance business, the policyholder is not only the final customer but also plays a significant role as a financier—though not overtly. An insurance company uses the principle of "float" provided by the policyholder to finance its business. Hence, insurance firms can be seen to have three major sources of funding—equity, debt, and float.

A policyholder pays regular premiums in order to secure an insurance cover. The likelihood of claims arising on a particular insurance cover is normally very low.[13] The insurance company enjoys the benefits of liquidity and funding provided by all its policyholders—the float arises on account of low probability of the risk ever happening plus the time gap between payment of premiums and the claim occurring, if at all.

The business model of insurance involves collecting premiums from policyholders and investing the cash into investments that appear on the assets side of the balance sheet. These investments and the returns therefrom have to be sufficient and available to make payments to policyholders in the case of a claim. The two main activities and sources of revenues for an insurance company therefore, are underwriting and investments.

Cash management is a critical activity in an insurance company. Cash is required for the firm's day-to-day operations as also to earn sufficiently to not only enable settling of future claims but also to generate profits and build reserves for the shareholders of the firm. The graphic in Figure 5.2 explains this trade-off the management has to deal with. Whether it is nonlife or life insurance, the essential business model remains same as depicted in the figure.

---

[13]The probability of claim is a complex calculation done by actuarial experts and varies across type of risk and context of risk. For example, risk of floods is greater in coastal areas than in landlocked cities.

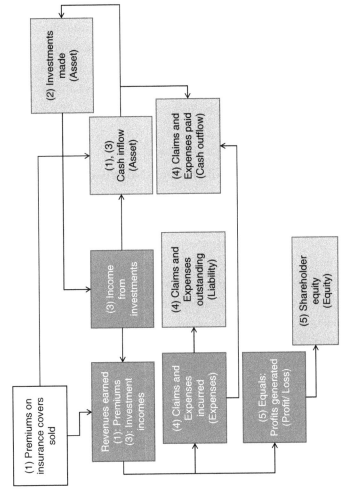

Figure 5.2 Mechanics of the insurance business

Notes: The numbers in the boxes represent the order in which the activities occur.

In India, the RBI and the Insurance Regulatory and Development Authority of India are the sector regulators for the banking and insurance sectors, respectively. These bodies decide on how the companies in the respective sectors should account for their business in the interest of due representation and disclosure. In the United States, the U.S. GAAP dictates the overarching accounting principles and conventions. The differences between IFRS and U.S. GAAP are several, in terms of principle. While this discussion is beyond the scope of this book, suffice it to say that these differences become starker when accounting for financial services firms than for nonfinancial services ones. However, irrespective of these differences and the formats, the business models can be read out of the financial statements.

Financial Statements of Nonlife Insurance Business

ICICI Lombard General Insurance Company Limited (ICICI Lombard)[14], under the umbrella of the financial services behemoth ICICI Bank, is one of India's leading nonlife insurance companies.

The reader will notice in the balance sheet of ICICI Lombard in Table 5.8 that its liabilities are dominated by shareholder equity and current liabilities; the largest components of the latter are liabilities to policyholders—claims outstanding and unallocated premium. As discussed earlier, shareholder equity and policyholder float are the primary sources of funding for insurance companies and market borrowings are not a necessary or even significant source of funds most often. Having said that, policyholder "funds" do not appear directly as a source of funds in nonlife insurance firms' balance sheets unlike for life insurance companies as we will see in the next section. The shareholders are the ultimate owners of the firm by virtue of being investors of risk capital and residual claimants of profits from the business. As in any other business, their funding appears as shareholder funds comprising share capital and free reserves.

The other largest item comprising current liabilities is balances owed to other insurance companies. This is primarily commission and claims

---

[14]Financial statements for ICICI Lombard sourced from the Draft Red Herring Prospectus (DRHP) dated July 14, 2017 put out by the company; http://www.ml-india.com/downloads/ICICILombardGeneralInsuranceCompanyLimitedDRHP.pdf

Table 5.8 Balance sheet for ICICI Lombard General Insurance Co. Ltd.

	For year ended on day of				
	March 31, 2017	**March 31, 2016**	**March 31, 2015**	**March 31, 2014**	**March 31, 2013**
Sources of funds					
Share capital	4,512	4,475	4,466	4,451	4,370
Reserves and surplus	32,752	27,879	24,389	19,486	14,327
Fair value change account					
Shareholders' funds	1,745	605	687	183	120
Policyholders' funds	5,027	2,485	2,872	952	580
Borrowings	4,850	–	–	–	–
Total liabilities	**48,886**	**35,445**	**32,414**	**25,071**	**19,397**
Application of funds					
Investments— Shareholders	39,826	23,886	20,888	15,081	12,889
Investments— Policyholders	110,963	91,739	81,110	77,819	65,111
Fixed assets	3,827	3,832	3,897	3,895	4,004
Deferred tax asset	873	1,239	969	351	485
Total noncurrent assets	155,489	120,696	106,863	97,146	82,489
Cash and bank balance	1,940	1,948	1,417	1,620	2,696
Advances and other assets	76,077	48,498	38,177	48,672	41,183
Total current assets	78,017	50,446	39,594	50,292	43,879
Less: Current liabilities					
Current liabilities	149,136	104,598	89,118	99,340	85,413
Provisions	35,485	31,100	24,925	23,026	21,558
Net current assets	(106,603)	(85,251)	(74,449)	(72,075)	(63,092)
Total assets	**48,886**	**35,445**	**32,414**	**25,071**	**19,397**

Note: Amounts are in INR million.

money to coinsurers or reinsurers. The asset side of ICICI Lombard's balance sheet is dominated by cash and investments. Advances are another large item into which an insurance company might deploy its cash in order to earn revenues. The other half of Figure 5.2 is reflected in the two statements—Revenue account and P&L statement—presented in Tables 5.9 and 5.10.

Table 5.9 Revenue account for ICICI Lombard General Insurance Co. Ltd.

	For year ended on day of				
	March 31, 2017	March 31, 2016	March 31, 2015	March 31, 2014	March 31, 2013
Premiums earned (net)	61,578	48,263	42,341	43,523	40,123
Net Profit on sale/ redemption of investments	2,970	2,704	1,754	1,217	575
Other income	269	483	315	215	146
Interest, dividend and rent	6,989	6,592	6,038	5,329	4,030
Gross revenues	71,805	58,043	50,448	50,284	44,874
Claims incurred (net)	49,656	39,391	34,456	36,289	33,502
Commission (net)	(4,341)	(3,280)	(3,463)	(2,291)	(1,831)
Operating expenses related to insurance business	19,820	17,112	13,871	12,158	10,194
Premium deficiency	–	–	–	–	(17)
Total expenses	65,135	53,223	44,864	46,156	41,847
Operating profit	6,670	4,820	5,584	4,128	3,027
Transfer to shareholders' account	6,670	4,820	5,584	4,128	3,027

Note: All amounts are in INR million.

Table 5.10 P&L account for ICICI Lombard General Insurance Co. Ltd.

	For year ended on day of				
	March 31, 2017	March 31, 2016	March 31, 2015	March 31, 2014	March 31, 2013
Fire insurance	996	1,104	448	622	395
Marine insurance	(150)	(284)	(294)	(250)	4
Miscellaneous insurance	5,824	4,000	5,430	3,757	2,629
1. Total operating profit from insurance operations	6,670	4,820	5,584	4,128	3,027
Interest, dividend and rent	2,205	1,605	1,470	1,121	1,000
Net Profit on sale/ redemption of investments	942	673	349	239	113
2. Income from investments	3,146	2,278	1,820	1,360	1,112
Interest income on tax refund	17	139	19	73	9
Profit/loss on sale of fixed assets	(22)	4	(23)	(23)	(9)
3. Other income	(5)	142	(4)	51	–
Total revenues	9,811	7,240	7,400	5,539	4,139
For diminution in value of investments	–	–	142	85	21
For doubtful debts	91	45	68	162	304
For recoverable under reinsurance contracts	(39)	(35)	11	(122)	235
4. Provisions	51	10	220	125	561
Operating expenses	688	182	126	52	27

(continued)

Table 5.10 (*continued*)

	For year ended on day of				
	March 31, 2017	March 31, 2016	March 31, 2015	March 31, 2014	March 31, 2013
Bad debt written off	–	–	2	27	38
Penalty and miscellaneous	–	1	5	1	–
5. Other expenses	688	183	133	80	64
Total operating expenses	739	192	352	205	625
EBIT	9,072	7,048	7,047	5,334	3,514
Interest on debentures	271	–	–	–	–
Profit before tax	8,801	7,048	7,047	5,334	3,514
Provision for taxation	2,383	1,995	1,194	134	(14)
Profit after tax	6,418	5,053	5,853	5,201	3,528

Note: All amounts are in INR million.

Unlike for other sectors studied so far, insurance companies have two statements (or accounts) that describe their operations during the period. The regulator for insurance firms in India requires them to put out a separate Revenue account that precedes the conventional P&L statement. Essentially, the former records operations that are strictly meant for providing the core insurance service for the policyholders and lays out the surplus or deficit arising therefrom. In other words, it can be described as the "Policyholders' Surplus and Deficit account." Any surplus arising from these operations is transferred to the equity shareholders' P&L account, out of which all other expenses and provisions that are not directly related to providing the core insurance service are provided for. The final profit or loss remaining at the end is the shareholders' surplus. Policyholders of a nonlife insurance company normally do not participate in any surplus or suffer any losses of the company. Therefore, all surplus belongs to the shareholders.

In case the Revenue account shows a deficit, the shareholders of the company are bound to transfer funds to the favor of the policyholders so as to make good the promise of the firm to them. Having two separate accounts makes the flow and result of operations of the firm clear and transparent. The revenue account in Table 5.9 is itself a summation of individual revenue accounts drawn up for each business line of the company such as fire, marine, natural calamity, etc. Premiums are the primary source of revenue for an insurance firm. The premiums include premiums received on reinsurance provided to other firms and net of premiums ceded to reinsurers for covering the insurance company's primary risk. Investments yield interest or dividend and capital gains. These are the other primary source of revenues for an insurance company as is evident from the Revenue account. Claims are the largest item of expense for an insurance business. The claims include claims paid as well as outstanding. They also include the claims on reinsurance accepted net of reinsurance ceded.

Over the years the insurance industry has become very competitive as also commoditized. Hence, selling and marketing of insurance has become a very important part of the business. Agents are employed or contracted to reach out to customers and sell insurance. Commission to agents is a significant expense item for an insurance company and has in recent years taken center stage both in strategic discussions of top managements of insurance firms as well as with the regulator. The negative figure against commission expenses indicates that for ICICI Lombard commission on reinsurance ceded, that is, liability (and hence, business) transferred to reinsurers, is greater than the sum of the direct commission it paid to its distributors and commission paid to other insurers who it had reinsured. However, the reader should realize that since the Revenue account in Table 5.9 is the sum of all individual revenue accounts, net commission expense is not necessarily negative for all the insurance lines of the company.

Each business has to incur operating expenses such as employee costs, administrative expenses as well as marketing expenses. Some of these are directly allocated expenses, while others are apportioned across businesses. What is, however, important is that the business has to be able to bear these expenses given the amount of revenue it generates. All these expenses can be reduced or negotiated if required but genuine claims of policyholders are sacrosanct. Therefore, the regulator has limited the operating expenses a business line can load on its revenue account. Any excess expense has to be borne by the shareholders. As depicted in Figure 5.2, the profit or loss on the revenue account that is transferred to the P&L statement "owned by" the shareholders is the excess of revenues (premiums plus investment revenues) over expenses (claims, commissions, and other operating expenses).

Not all countries require the Revenue account and P&L statement to be drawn up separately. In the U.S. for instance, insurance firms provide a single P&L statement that lays out both sets of operations together. The revenues begin with premiums received across various lines of insurance as well as income from investments and other sources. Expenses include all expenses relating directly to the insurance operations and others too. The final surplus or deficit is the profit or loss respectively for the shareholders.

Once the surplus or deficit from the Revenue account is transferred to the P&L statement, this surplus forms the "top-line" for the shareholders as shown in Table 5.10. All revenues and expenses not accounted for in the Revenue accounts find place in the P&L statement. The shareholders are clearly the claimants to all residual incomes and liable for all expenses not loaded on the individual businesses, including interest on debt.

The reader will notice investment income forming part of the P&L statement as well. What investments are these that "belong" to the shareholders and not to the policyholders, in a manner of speaking? An insurance company can invest cash received from two primary sources—premium receipts and cash "belonging" to the shareholders by virtue of their equity contribution, which includes profits retained in business. Of course, it is not possible to identify *which cash* has come from either source. Therefore, it becomes necessary to apportion investments between policyholders and shareholders. In nonlife insurance business where the firm owes the policyholders only to the extent of their claims, the firm needs to apportion investments only to suffice this requirement. Indian insurance firms are mandated to make this apportionment in the ratio of policyholders' funds to shareholders' funds. This takes us to the question of what constitutes shareholders' funds and what the components of policyholders' funds are. The definition of shareholders' funds is just the same as in any business—share capital and free reserves. Policyholders' funds, simply put, is the amount that the firm owes to the policyholders as on the balance sheet date. These amounts form part of the item Current Liabilities in the balance sheet. The reader should note that current liabilities form the largest component of the liabilities side of ICICI Lombard's balance sheet. Of the INR 149 billion of current liabilities at the end of FY2017, over INR 127 billion or 85 percent was owed to policyholders. Shareholder funds formed around 25 percent of shareholder and policyholder funds put together.

Returning to the P&L statement, the last significant item is Provisions. The insurance company has to make provisions for advances that may turn bad, similar to banks if it is into lending. But more important, they have to make provisions for diminution in the value of their investments. For commercial banks, lending was the primary activity, while investment was secondary. This is completely reversed in the case of insurance firms.

The 4-way DuPont framework could not be applied to commercial banks since interest expenses were operating in nature or rather it was difficult to segregate the interest expense arising on account of financing activities. However, this is not a problem in the case of insurance business. Although the customer—the policyholder—is also a primary financier as she provides float, the returns to the policyholder are not in the form of interest; they are the claims on her cover and these are clearly operating expenses.[15] Similar to a customer in any other goods or services business, the policyholder pays the insurance firm the premium for providing her a service of an insurance cover and honoring her claim, if any.

Table 5.11 DuPont analysis for ICICI Lombard

	Year Ended 31st Day of			
	March 31, 2017	March 31, 2016	March 31, 2015	March 31, 2014
Interest burden	4.05%	–	–	–
NOPAT margin	8.93%	8.36%	11.20%	10.06%
ATR	0.37	0.38	0.36	0.38
LEV	5.81	5.19	5.57	6.42
ROE	18.44%	16.51%	22.18%	24.40%
ROA from operations	3.31%	3.18%	3.98%	3.80%

---

[15]The reader should note that when leverage is computed as Assets/ Equity, it includes liabilities that may not attract explicit interest costs. They may incur certain implicit costs that get subsumed in the operating expenses and hence, get reflected in the NOPAT margin rather than in RES. This scenario especially stands out in the case of firms that have low amounts of financial debt such as TCS and ICICI Lombard.

As evident from Table 5.11, return to equity holders (ROE) has clearly been reducing for the company; it is too early to say whether FY2017 is showing a reversal. However, the ROE by itself is not too low and indicates reasonable performance. Of the 18.44 percent ROE for FY2017, ROA comprises only 3.31 percent and it is financial leverage that has amplified return for equity holders. This is quite similar to the case of the commercial banking business. The definition of leverage used in the DuPont analysis is Assets divided by Equity, which means all external liabilities—not necessarily debt raised for financing activity—are included in leverage. This is different from the regular debt-to-equity ratio that normally includes only actively raised debt (liabilities arising on account of business activity including operating current liabilities, pension liabilities, etc. are excluded). In the case of banks, leverage largely comprised deposits; market borrowings were not necessary or could be insignificant. In the case of insurance business similarly, leverage is driven by current liabilities; market borrowings are normally not a significant or necessary funding route for insurance companies. So essentially, the numerator is dominated by policyholder funds. Therefore, leverage is quite close to the ratio of policyholder funds to shareholder funds. Of course, as seen earlier, current liabilities also include amounts owed to agents and other service providers in the system.

It is interesting to see that ICICI Lombard's leverage has been falling consistently over the years and seems to have increased slightly in FY2017 only because of the long-term borrowings. Everything else being the same, this points to an accumulation of shareholder equity faster than the growth in policyholder funds. Is this good news or bad news or is it too soon to say?

Accumulation of shareholder funds is a healthy sign as it indicates greater net accumulation of operating (and maybe, other) surplus into shareholder reserves. The NOPAT margin has also been showing a declining trend, albeit a slight uptick is visible in FY2017. So the accumulation of shareholder reserves cannot be attributed to improving operations either. Before we go any further, it is important to see how the peculiarities of the insurance business influence the DuPont analysis and what kind of digging can help an inquisitive analyst.

What definition of revenues can best serve the purpose of this analysis? As done for all other businesses, revenues can be picked up from the P&L

statement, for example, for FY2017 it is INR 9,811 million. But does this really represent the starting point? The role of revenues in computation of ATR is to determine how well assets have been utilized to generate business. The numbers that depict business generation from underwriting can be found in the Revenue account. So we should ideally take the top-line of INR 71,805 million for FY2017 and add to it all nonunderwriting revenues generated in the P&L statement—investment income on shareholders' account and other income. This viewpoint of business opens up an entirely new window to understanding how the business has been performing. On the underwriting business, the company's margin performance had been improving until FY2015 (work out the operating margins on the revenue accounts), after which a steep decline was followed by a slight uptick. Underwriting operating margins stood at 9.3 percent for FY2017. This net result of underwriting gets transferred to the P&L statement to form the top-line for shareholders. Over the 5 years, the share of underwriting in gross revenues in the P&L statement had been steadily decreasing from 73 percent in FY2013 to 68 percent in FY2017.

While investment is as much a core part of the business model of insurance as is underwriting, it would not be wrong to say that underwriting is still the primary one. The essential business of the firm is to underwrite risks. The margins earned by an insurance company will be a composition of margins from both these businesses. Strictly speaking, profitability on investment activity is limited by the trend in interest rates and yields as also regulations applicable to these companies. Unlike companies purely engaged in investment activity, insurance firms' investment choices are regulated to ensure that they do not take on more than a certain measure of risk for the sake of higher returns. Therefore, consistent growth in underwriting business is not only required to maintain or improve margins[16] but also indicates market share maintenance and/or

---

[16]While insurance is a highly competitive and commoditized market, margins can be worked upon by better pricing of risk with a view on possible claims as also by optimizing other costs that yield economies of scale and scope. Commissions are a function of the sales strategy the firm adopts and it is an area an insurance company can come up with innovative methods to yield maximum premium income per rupee of commission. Incentives and metrics used for measuring performance or to drive a certain type of performance play a significant role in insurance underwriting.

growth of the firm in the insurance market. Single digit NOPAT margins will need to be improved in order to get the ROA up.

Finally, is ATR of between 35 percent and 40 percent good enough? In commercial banking we saw that ATR was limited by the interest rates prevailing in the market and unless a bank took on unduly risky credits, ATR of, say, 15 percent, was also a difficult target in the Indian market. This was because the assets deployed were largely deposits. In the case of a nonlife insurance business, assets deployed are predominantly investments (and advances too in the case of ICICI Lombard). This is very similar to the case of a bank where every rupee invested or lent out can yield only a certain amount in the form of income limited by the yields prevailing in the market (besides movement of yields, the timing and classification of investments plays an important role in capital gains/losses from investments). In fact, the average return on investment on shareholder investments and policyholder investments[17] ranges between 7 percent and 10 percent for ICICI Lombard. This clearly shows that the ATR of over 35 percent is largely attributable to the underwriting business. This is one more reason for the insurance company to focus more on underwriting risks.

Finally, turning our attention to the CFS in Table 5.12, we notice that the format in which the CFO has been drawn up for ICICI Lombard is somewhat different from the standard "indirect method" that was used for all previous examples. In fact, the format used here to arrive at the CFO is the direct method.[18] In the case of banks, the reader would recollect, that the CFS does not provide much incremental information of value unlike nonfinance businesses that were studied in previous chapters. Therefore, it is important to see if the CFS of an insurance firm is any more useful, irrespective of format.

The CFS shows a significant jump in cash flows in FY2017 from the previous year. CFO has tripled, while CFI has gone up sixfold and the

---

[17]Return on investments "belonging" to policyholders is computed as sum of net profit/loss from sale or redemption of investments and interest, dividend, rent from investments, both taken from the revenue account, as a percentage of average investments apportioned to policyholders. The same figures are picked up from the P&L statement to compute return on investments to shareholders.

[18]American insurers follow the standard indirect method format that is used for non-financial services firms.

Table 5.12 Cash flow statements for ICICI Lombard

	For year ended on day of				
	March 31, 2017	**March 31, 2016**	**March 31, 2015**	**March 31, 2014**	**March 31, 2013**
Premium from PHs, incl. advance receipts	103,976	88,077	73,526	71,676	65,679
Other receipts*	537	560	255	242	170
Net receipts from reinsurer**	(5,645)	(5,835)	4,054	(2,211)	2,880
Net receipts from coinsurers#	2,940	1,878	1,046	2,695	409
Payments of claims (net of salvage)	(49,938)	(49,416)	(56,174)	(44,210)	(41,795)
Payment of commission and brokerage	(5,201)	(4,207)	(3,771)	(3,738)	(3,056)
Payment of operating expenses	(20,926)	(17,665)	(13,823)	(12,717)	(9,595)
Net deposits, advances, staff loans	(168)	61	(171)	(97)	936
Income tax paid (net)	(1,969)	(1,812)	(1,234)	(885)	(602)
Service tax paid	(7,329)	(6,528)	(4,686)	(4,806)	(5,184)
Cash from operating activities	**16,278**	**5,114**	**(979)**	**5,949**	**9,842**
Net purchase of fixed assets	(535)	(523)	(516)	(383)	(500)
Purchase of investments	(138,143)	(80,314)	(83,741)	(108,635)	(92,436)
Sale of investments	116,769	69,270	78,509	98,891	73,434
Rent/interest/dividends received	7,793	7,200	6,821	5,835	4,278

(continued)

Table 5.12 (continued)

	For year ended on day of				
	March 31, 2017	March 31, 2016	March 31, 2015	March 31, 2014	March 31, 2013
ST and liquid investments (net)	(5,761)	1,284	1,599	(2,677)	5,617
Other cash flow from investments (net)	(23)	(16)	(961)	(96)	(19)
Cash from investing activities	**(19,899)**	**(3,099)**	**1,711**	**(7,064)**	**(9,625)**
Proceeds from issue of equity capital	381	62	121	39	1,022
Net proceeds from borrowing	4,829	–	–	–	–
Interest/ dividends paid	(1,597)	(1,547)	(1,056)	–	–
Cash from financing activities	**3,613**	**(1,485)**	**(935)**	**39**	**1,022**
Net increase/ decrease in cash	(8)	531	(203)	(1,077)	1,239
Cash and cash equivalents at beginning	1,948	1,417	1,620	2,696	1,457
Cash and cash equivalents at end	1,940	1,948	1,417	1,620	2,696

Notes: All figures in INR million.
*Includes Motor TP pool and terrorism pool.
**Net of claims recovery and commissions.
#Net of claims recovery.

firm has seen a threefold rise in cash inflows from financing, taking the net cash flow from financing from negative INR 1.5 billion to a positive INR 3.6 billion in FY2017. Neither the balance sheet nor the revenue account or P&L statement of FY2017 shows such stark jumps in scale.

CFS of FY2016, similarly, shows significant cash flow movement compared to the previous year. This in itself makes the study of ICICI Lombard's CFS an interesting study.

In FY2017 the insurer's receipts on account of premiums were over 160 percent of the net premiums earned. The gap is clearly premiums received in advance and unearned premiums that formed part of the insurer's current liabilities and policyholders' funds. All the five years show receipts greater than premium earnings, which is normal for a growing business. In fact, in FY2016 and FY2015, premium receipts were more than 180 percent and 170 percent, respectively, of premium earnings. Similarly, a large gap of more than 20 percent can be observed between commission and brokerage incurred and paid for all the years excepting one with payments being greater than incurrence. Clearly, distributors are significant partners for insurers and indeed they form the most important set of service providers for an insurance business.

Financial securities dominate the investment activity for an insurance company, with investment in fixed assets being almost insignificant in comparison. Unlike nonfinance businesses discussed earlier, the operations of an insurance business are reflected not only in its cash from operating activities but also in its cash from investment activities. In other words, while the underwriting side of its business is reflected predominantly in its CFO, the investment side of its business dominates its CFI. It may be worth pondering whether cash flows involving financial investments should be part of CFI or CFO as for an insurance firm investment in financial assets is part of their core business model. Then how should free cash flow be defined for an insurance business? How should it be interpreted? The objectives of the analyst should ideally drive the answers to these questions.

Since policyholder funds are a significant source of funds for an insurance firm and become bigger in scale as the firm grows, cash flows from financing (CFF) comparatively lose significance in providing any information of relevance.

Finally, it is important to mention some of the important metrics or ratios that define the performance of a general insurance business (Table 5.13).

Table 5.13 Important ratios for general insurance business

	For year ended on day of				
	March 31, 2017	March 31, 2016	March 31, 2015	March 31, 2014	March 31, 2013
Claims ratio or loss ratio	0.81	0.82	0.81	0.83	0.83
Expense ratio	0.25	0.29	0.25	0.23	0.21
Combined ratio	1.06	1.10	1.06	1.06	1.04
Underwriting profit ratio	(5.78)%	(10.28)%	(5.96)%	(6.05)%	(4.30)%
Operating profit ratio	10.83%	9.99%	13.19%	9.49%	7.54%

Claims ratio is simply the claims incurred in the year divided by the premiums earned during the year. More than 80 percent of the premiums earned[19] are paid or liable to be paid as claims to policyholders, leaving less than 20 percent of the primary revenue source for other expenses and return to the equity holders. Insurance business works on the law of large numbers and randomness of events. The pricing of an insurance cover builds into it the probability of loss occurring on a cover and the larger the universe covered the more predictable the model becomes and better the pricing. The expense ratio is the ratio of the commission and operating expenses together as percentage of the premiums earned.

Claims, commissions, and operating expenses include practically all costs of running an underwriting business. The combined ratio captures this comprehensive reality and provides a quick view of what can be left for the shareholders. A combined ratio of more than 100 percent clearly shows that underwriting business has no surplus to offer and in fact, has been dipping into investment revenues. This is also reflected in the negative underwriting profit ratio. On the other hand, a close to 11 percent operating profit ratio—defined as sum of underwriting and investment

---

[19]Depending on the regulations of the land, the actual formulation used can differ from gross or net premium written or earned. The essence of providing these numbers is to understand the business of insurance through these ratios, even if they differ marginally from the strict calculations required by the regulators.

profits divided by premiums earned—shows the contribution of investment income not only in holding up the promise to policyholders but also in generating surplus for shareholders.

Financial Statements of a Life Insurance Firm

The business model of insurance remains the same for life insurance as seen for general insurance. The differences arise on account of the basic nature of the risk that is insured—objects in general insurance versus life in the case of life insurance. The primary difference in the way insurance is therefore viewed in both cases is that objects such as motor vehicle or household goods, etc. may or may not suffer damage but life is definitely finite. What does this mean for the insurer? In the former case, claim on a cover is uncertain in terms of occurrence, timing, and quantum, while in the case of life insurance occurrence of the event and sum assured is certain, the uncertain factor is only the timing. In that sense, the company can work with greater predictability and less random variables in deciding product and pricing. Second, the policyholder may be exposed to the covered risk only for a limited period of time in the case of general insurance, while in the case of life the exposure lasts until death. For example, in the case of motor vehicle insurance, once the vehicle is sold off and in the case of travel insurance once the travel is completed, the need for insurance expires. Therefore, in the case of general insurance, each "renewal" of insurance is also treated as a new cover. However, in the case of life insurance, the company looks at the lifetime of the individual from a cost, return, and service perspective. Retention of a policyholder therefore, takes a very different complexion making it priority in the case of life insurance.

Let us begin with the financial statements that resemble those of non-life insurance business. Birla Sun Life Insurance Company[20] is the life insurance business of the Aditya Birla Capital group, its holding company and is a joint venture between ABC group and Sun Life Financial Inc. of Canada and is one of the leading private life insurers in India.

---

[20]Financial statements for Birla Sun Life Insurance Co. sourced from the official website of Aditya Birla Sun Life Co. Ltd.

The basic business model as described in Figure 5.2 is evident in Table 5.14—sources of income are primarily premiums and investment income, and expenses comprise mainly benefits paid, commission expenses, and operating expenses. However, the differences between the Policyholders' account above and the Revenue account in the case of nonlife insurance are important. First, while ICICI Lombard paid out claims, Birla Sun Life pays out benefits. Life insurance[21] is larger in scope than nonlife insurance. Besides a vanilla term cover that resembles a nonlife cover, life insurance firms offer insurance policies of finite terms after which the policies mature. They also provide insurance-cum-investment instruments that pay out regular annuities. Thus, benefits include death claims, maturity payments, annuities as well as payouts when policies are closed out before maturity. Payouts on premature surrender of insurance cover forms the largest component of the benefits in the policyholders' account, which indicates two important features of life insurance. The most obvious one is that retaining policyholders for the life of the policy is not easy and hence, becomes an important metric to track and work toward for life insurance firms. Second, in insurance products other than simple term insurance, the premiums paid are not simply to cover the risk of death during that year; they are also at least partly, toward investment. Therefore, when a policyholder suspends paying premiums after a certain number of installments, she still has a claim on the firm and has to be returned some part of the past premiums paid.

The second important difference are two similar looking items in the Policyholders' account—"Gain/loss on revaluation or change in fair value" as an income and "Change in valuation of policy liabilities" as an expense. Unlike nonlife insurance, in life insurance, some investments are held specifically against "linked" policies, which are insurance-cum-investment products. In case of such policies, while the insurer is responsible for honoring the insurance cover in the event of death or maturity, the investment part can well be market-linked, that is, the policyholder bears the risk on it. Therefore, the premiums paid by the policyholder

[21]In the case of life, the correct term used is "assurance" and not "insurance." Loss of life cannot be strictly compensated for or replaced; what an insurance firm can do is provide assurance to the extent of the sum assured to the beneficiaries of the policyholder upon his/her death.

Table 5.14 Policyholders' account for Birla Sun Life

	For year ended on day of				
	March 31, 2017	March 31, 2016	March 31, 2015	March 31, 2014	March 31, 2013
Premiums earned (net)	55.34	54.12	50.68	46.45	50.52
Net profit on sale/ redemption of investments	10.46	8.67	29.15	2.99	6.39
Interest, dividend and rent	17.85	16.11	13.52	11.76	10.93
Gain/loss on revaluation/ change in fair value	15.07	(18.34)	10.42	10.21	3.39
Miscellaneous income	0.33	0.35	0.34	0.37	0.37
Contribution from shareholders' account	1.63	3.27	3.15	2.59	2.00
Gross revenues	100.67	64.16	107.27	74.36	73.58
Benefits paid (net)	46.52	42.47	37.72	36.66	36.59
Change in valuation of policy liabilities	39.62	6.01	53.07	21.13	17.99
Commission (net)	2.55	2.18	2.33	2.35	3.01
Operating expenses related to insurance business	8.69	10.04	9.73	10.37	11.60
Total expenses	97.39	60.71	102.85	70.50	69.18
Surplus	**3.29**	**3.46**	**4.42**	**3.86**	**4.40**
Transfer to shareholders' account	3.35	3.51	4.97	5.23	6.27

Note: All amounts in INR billion.

are invested in clearly earmarked investments rather than in a general pool. These investments are marked to market (MtM) or reported at fair value depending on their type (HTM or held for trading). Any gain or loss on such revaluations adds to the income pool of policyholders. The moment a life insurer accepts premium against an insurance cover, it takes on a liability. This liability requires constant evaluation based on multiple factors such as future cash flows from underlying investments, prevailing and expected rates of returns, probability of claim or surrender, etc. An increase in such liability essentially reduces surplus leftover for shareholders and, hence, appears along with expenses in the Policyholder's account. The size of both these items in proportion to the total income and expenses, respectively, provides an indication of the large quantum of investments a life insurance company maintains and toward the split of these investments between policyholders and shareholders.

The third important difference the reader might notice is that there is a contribution from shareholders to policyholders that adds to the income in the account and there is a transfer of surplus from the policyholders' account to the shareholders' account. However, unlike nonlife insurance, the latter is not exactly equal to the surplus remaining in the policyholders' account—in fact, it has always been greater in all the 5 years for Birla Sun Life. This entire process can be understood if one looks at the net transfer to/from one set of stakeholders to the other in Table 5.15.

The figures in Table 5.15 show the net amount that has been transferred to the shareholders from the policyholders' account in each of the

Table 5.15 Net surplus transferred to shareholders

	For year ended on day of				
	March 31, 2017	March 31, 2016	March 31, 2015	March 31, 2014	March 31, 2013
Net transfer to shareholders = Net Surplus for policyholders across business segments	1.72	0.24	1.81	2.63	4.27

Note: All figures are in INR billion.

5 years. The fundamental premise remains the same as was in nonlife insurance—any surplus in the policyholders' accounts after providing for all amounts due to the policyholders, is transferred to the shareholders' account. In the case of life insurance too, surplus or deficit is computed under each business segment—linked and nonlinked policies, participating and nonparticipating policies—and the sum of such surplus/deficit is the net amount that should go to the credit of the shareholders' account. This surplus/deficit is as shown in Table 5.15. Therefore, the final transfer to shareholders' account is a sum that makes a net transfer of such surplus/deficit to the shareholders' account.

Table 5.16 *P&L statements for Birla Sun Life*

	For year ended on day of				
	March 31, 2017	March 31, 2016	March 31, 2015	March 31, 2014	March 31, 2013
Amount transferred from Policyholders' account	3.35	3.51	4.97	5.23	6.27
Income from investments	1.49	1.49	1.28	1.15	1.16
Total income	4.84	5.00	6.24	6.38	7.43
Expenses other than directly related to insurance business	1.98	0.33	0.24	0.07	0.02
Provisions	–	–	–	–	–
Contribution to Policyholders' account	1.63	3.27	3.15	2.59	2.00
Total expenses	3.61	3.60	3.39	2.67	2.01
Profit before tax	1.23	1.40	2.85	3.71	5.42
Provision for taxation	–	–	–	–	–
Profit after tax	1.23	1.40	2.85	3.71	5.42

Note: All figures are in INR billion.

As in the case of nonlife insurance companies, the P&L statement (Table 5.16) is the shareholders' account and the first item of income is the surplus transferred from the policyholders' account. Income from investments—interest, dividends and capital gains/losses—comprises the other item of income for the shareholders. Expenses include operating expenses not allocated or apportioned to insurance business segments and provisions. The other important item of expenses is contribution from shareholders' to policyholders' account that appeared as an item of income in the latter. The resulting profit adds up to the free reserves in shareholder funds on the balance sheet.

Table 5.17 Balance sheets for Birla Sun Life

	For year ended on day of				
	March 31, 2017	March 31, 2016	March 31, 2015	March 31, 2014	March 31, 2013
Sources of funds					
Share capital	19.01	19.01	19.01	19.01	19.70
Reserves and surplus	2.68	2.68	2.68	2.68	4.80
Debit balance in P&L account	(3.65)	(4.88)	(6.28)	(9.13)	(12.02)
Balance in fair value change account	(0.00)	(0.00)	–	0.00	–
Shareholder funds	18.05	16.82	15.42	12.57	12.48
Balance in fair value change account	0.25	(0.26)	0.34	0.04	(0.00)
Policy liabilities	84.60	59.64	42.86	28.35	20.30
Total linked liabilities	248.88	234.23	245.01	206.45	193.37
Total policyholder funds	333.73	293.61	288.21	234.84	213.67
Funds for future appropriation (linked liabilities)	0.07	0.13	0.19	0.73	2.10
Total equity and liabilities	351.85	310.56	303.81	248.14	228.24

Table 5.17 (*continued*)

	For year ended on day of				
	March 31, 2017	March 31, 2016	March 31, 2015	March 31, 2014	March 31, 2013
Application of funds					
Investments					
Shareholders'	16.04	17.07	15.52	13.29	13.71
Policyholders'	80.31	56.82	41.31	28.01	22.22
Assets held to cover linked liabilities	248.88	234.23	245.01	206.45	193.37
Loans	0.54	0.48	0.38	0.29	0.28
Fixed assets	0.81	0.65	0.49	0.40	0.34
Total noncurrent assets	346.58	309.24	302.72	248.43	229.92
Cash and bank balances	4.99	4.81	4.31	5.08	5.44
Advances and other assets	8.30	5.01	3.88	3.54	3.07
Total current assets	13.29	9.82	8.19	8.62	8.51
Less: Current liabilities	7.77	8.27	6.82	7.79	8.57
Provisions	0.25	0.23	0.28	1.12	1.61
Net current assets	5.27	1.33	1.09	(0.29)	(1.68)
Total assets	**351.85**	**310.56**	**303.81**	**248.14**	**228.24**

Note: All figures are in INR billion.

As seen for a nonlife insurance firm, the reader will observe in the balance sheet in Table 5.17 that the assets of a life insurer are also dominated by investments; fixed assets form a negligible portion in comparison. The difference, however, is the way policyholder funds are represented and conveyed. While in ICICI Lombard all policyholder liabilities formed part of the firm's current liabilities, in the case of a life insurer, policyholder funds are shown separately as liabilities owed to them and corresponding investments set aside clearly on the assets side of the balance sheet.

Since in life insurance, policyholders holding market-linked products partake in the investment risk, it behooves the insurer to keep investments purchased using their monies separately and report them clearly in the financial statements. The reader will note identical figures of INR 248.88 billion on both the assets and liabilities side of the balance sheet ended FY2017. The liabilities on account of linked insurance covers require the firm to earmark investments of equivalent value against them. Separate fund level revenue accounts and balance sheets are maintained for each linked product and surpluses/deficit arising on their account are added to the reserves accruing to the contributing policyholders. The firm is only responsible for the risk cover on account of life insured in these cases and not for investment returns or bonuses that are part of the product.

While it has been clearly established that investments are the most important asset component for insurers, their dominance and importance is quite different between nonlife and life insurers. While investments form only about 65 percent of total assets for the former, they comprise nearly 97 percent of total assets for the latter! Naturally, management of investments takes a very different complexion for life insurance firms. On the liabilities side of the balance sheet, the importance of policyholders as providers of finance also similarly changes in importance. While the policyholders' funds were more than three times shareholder funds for ICICI Lombard, in the case of Birla Sun Life, they are over 18 times shareholder funds! In India, most life insurance products sold are investment-cum-insurance products, though this trend is now slowly changing with customers going to insurance firms for pure term insurance and looking at alternative avenues such as mutual funds for their investment needs. Investment products yield greater premiums, which add up to the policyholder liabilities as well as corresponding investments.

Birla Sun Life's shareholder funds comprise an item of debit balance in the P&L statement, which clearly indicates accumulated losses. The good news though is that this debit balance has been steadily reducing over the years, thanks to surpluses being generated for shareholders over these years.

So how well has the firm performed for its shareholders? The DuPont analysis in Table 5.18 provides the answers.

While the firm has been making profits every successive year over the last 5 years, it clearly does not seem enough to provide consistent

Table 5.18 *DuPont analysis for Birla Sun Life*

	For year ended on day of			
	March 31, 2017	March 31, 2016	March 31, 2015	March 31, 2014
Interest burden	–	–	–	–
NOPAT margin	2.24%	2.71%	5.09%	7.44%
ATR	0.18	0.33	0.26	0.29
LEV	19.47	19.54	20.29	19.79
ROE	8.03%	17.71%	26.51%	43.25%
ROA from operations	0.41%	0.91%	1.31%	2.19%

shareholder returns. Both ROA and ROE have been sliding over the period under study. Both profit margins and ATR seem to have been contributing to this slide in ROA. Let us look at each one by turns.

With investments not just dominating but almost comprising the total assets of a life insurer, the returns on investments will dictate the asset utilization of such a business. While interest and dividend incomes tend to be smoother as can be seen in the policyholder's account, capital gains and losses on sale and marking to market tend to be very volatile. With the latter being a substantial amount either way, ATR of a life insurer tends to be a function of the market movements and the ability of fund managers to respond to it. Another important factor is the pattern of inflows into and outflows from the funds. When policyholders decide to terminate a policy or when a policy matures, the fund managers sell investments backing the policyholders' liabilities in order to make payments to them. If such redemptions happen when markets are at a low, the fund will book losses on sale of investments. Portfolio management skills, therefore, become very crucial in this business.

As for control of the firm over its operating margins, interestingly, unlike other businesses, while the firm may have control over its costs, it is its lack of control over the revenue line that seems to cause the volatility in NOPAT margins. Margins dipped perceptibly in FY2016. Clearly, these can be attributed to revenues dipping from INR 105bn to INR 62bn in FY2016. This dip can be almost completely attributed to the loss on revaluation of INR 18bn in the year as against gains of INR 10bn in the previous 2 years. With a volatile ROA, ROE too is quite volatile for a life insurer whose top-line is investment income driven. As policyholder funds make up all the financial leverage in the system and are over 18 times shareholder funds, ROA gets amplified by over 19 times when converted to ROE! This also means that if the precariously positioned ROA of 0.41 percent dips into the negative zone, shareholders will be faced with a blown-up negative ROE on their funds.[22] So how does a business like Birla Sun Life bring more predictability into its performance metrics?

As seen for a nonlife insurer, for a life-insurance firm too, underwriting revenues are more predictable and controllable compared to investment revenues. With term insurance picking up in preference among Indian youth, we may see a shift in business more towards underwriting than investment and in composition of assets in some years. Of course, premiums are far lower in vanilla term insurance, so it will play out in multiple ways. Insurance business, especially insurance on life, rests crucially on the actuarial capabilities present in the firm. Predicting underwriting inflows and outflows better will help firms plan their investments better. Of course, with interest rates dipping and close to zero in most countries (India's 10-year government bond yields still trade at 7 percent or upwards), investment income will become more vulnerable to market movements and smart fund management will take center stage.

The CFS in Table 5.19 is quite like what was encountered in the nonlife insurance case. Premiums received and benefits disbursed, which define the underwriting business, dominate the cash flows from operations. Income from investments, whether by way of interest and dividends or by way of capital gains and losses, is classified under cash flows from investments. Fixed assets investments, too, find their place in this category. Cash flows on account of capital gains and losses are not explicitly mentioned as they are ensconced in the purchases and sale of investments. Fair value adjustments on account of marking to market are noncash adjustments that do

---

[22]As seen for nonlife insurance, here too, the financial leverage does not attract interest liability. The cost of leverage is incorporated in the operating expenses and gets reflected in NOPAT margin. Hence, the 4-way DuPont model does not play out as explained in Chapter 2.

Table 5.19 Cash flow statements for Birla Sun Life

	For year ended on day of			
	March 31, 2017	**March 31, 2016**	**March 31, 2015**	**March 31, 2014**
Premium from PHs, incl. advance receipts	57.05	55.98	51.62	47.90
Net receipts from reinsurer	(0.54)	(0.54)	(0.27)	(0.65)
Other deposits, receipts	0.14	0.27	0.35	0.40
Payments of claims (net of salvage)	(50.11)	(43.57)	(39.19)	37.88)
Payment of commission and brokerage	(2.43)	(2.18)	(2.37)	(2.37)
Payment of operating expenses	(10.91)	(6.57)	(10.17)	(11.16)
Taxes paid	(0.85)	–	–	–
Cash from operating activities	**(7.65)**	**3.39**	**(0.02)**	**(3.75)**
Net purchase of fixed assets	(0.47)	(0.45)	(0.32)	(0.29)
Purchase of investments	(2,170.46)	(1,798.21)	(1,769.65)	(2,133.51)
Sale of investments	2,161.72	1,780.58	1,757.48	2,130.15
Loans against policies and other loans	(0.01)	(0.06)	(0.06)	0.02
Interest/dividends/rent from investments (net)	17.04	15.25	12.61	11.20
Cash from investing activities	**7.83**	**(2.88)**	**0.07**	**7.57**
Proceeds from issue of equity capital	–	–	–	(2.80)
Interest/dividends paid	–	–	(0.82)	(1.38)
Cash from financing activities	**–**	**–**	**(0.82)**	**(4.18)**
Net increase/decrease in cash	0.18	0.51	(0.78)	(0.37)
Cash and cash equivalents at beginning	4.81	4.30	5.07	5.44
Cash and cash equivalents at end	4.99	4.81	4.30	5.07

Note: All figures are in INR billion.

not figure in the CFS. What is important to understand and probably question, is whether activities relating to financial investments should be part of CFI or CFO. Do these not constitute regular operations of an insurer? As discussed in the previous section, this applies to both nonlife and life insurers. This becomes material when one is looking at free cash flow generation from a business. Free cash flows, the reader will recollect, are cash flows from operations less capital expenditures. Therefore, for purposes of analysis, it may well serve if cash flows from financial investments are added to cash flows from operations to understand strength of cash flows of the firm. Of course, this applies only to investments meant to provide returns and insurance covers to policyholders and not investments made using shareholder funds. Now, segregating the two is easier said than done!

Besides the performance ratios that form part of the DuPont analysis, there are at least two ratios shown in Table 5.20 that are peculiar to and important for life insurance businesses.

Unlike nonlife insurance, lifetime value per customer takes precedence and meaning in the case of life insurance. Hence, retention of a customer becomes very important if such value has to accrue to the business and its shareholders. Second, in the financial services businesses, such as insurance and mutual funds management, thanks to high competition and low margins, acquiring a customer is an expensive proposition. The 13th month persistency ratio indicates that 71.45 percent of its new policyholders pay up the first renewal premium to keep the policy alive (renewal premiums are typically annual). The firm has made perceptible improvement on this front over the 4 years.[23] However, retaining a customer for

Table 5.20 *Some more performance ratios for Birla Sun Life*

	For year ended on day of			
	March 31, 2017	March 31, 2016	March 31, 2015	March 31, 2014
Persistency ratio—13th month	71.45%	64.69%	62.17%	60.10%
Persistency ratio—61st month	47.05%	35.45%	38.87%	43.50%
Solvency ratio	2.00	2.11	2.05	1.86

---

[23]Many life insurers are encouraging their distributors to push single premium policies where renewal is not required. This could be the result of low persistency ratios in the past and the reason for improvement in persistency in recent years.

5 years is a stretch and, while 43.5 percent customers continued after 5 years since inception at the end of FY2014, this number declined to 35.45 percent 2 years later. However, the firm seems to have managed to significantly bring this number up to over 47 percent at the end of FY2017, that is, of the new policyholders who signed up in FY2012, more than 47 percent continued to pay their premiums at least until the end of FY2017. A comparison of persistency ratios across firms can give an indication of customer satisfaction across firms.

The solvency ratio is much like the CRAR (capital adequacy ratio) encountered in the case of banks. Unlike normal businesses, banks and insurance companies cannot simply fail without causing systemic ripples. They hold small deposits and investments of the public and provide either an implicit or explicit guarantee of safety and/or returns on such monies. Hence, they need to hold equity sufficient to cover any risk of some of the assets into which these monies are invested, going bad. The insurance regulator in India has imposed a solvency margin of 150 percent of assets over insurance liabilities.[24] The solvency ratio is defined as the actual margin held divided by the required margin. Table 5.20 indicates that Birla Sun Life has more than twice the required margin of assets as required by the regulator. But does this indeed make the policyholders' guarantees safe? Recently, one of India's insurers with the highest solvency ratios, Sahara Life, that posted a solvency ratio of over eight times, went bankrupt and its assets and liabilities were acquired by another private sector insurer. At the time of writing this book, the IRDAI was working on redesigning the solvency margin requirements to better align them to the risk of the insurer's liabilities.

To conclude, financial services are a unique set of businesses where money is not a means but the end itself. Cash is resource and cash is inventory. The customer is the revenue provider as well as a primary provider of funding, whether as a depositor placing deposits with a bank or as a policyholder providing float. Financial leverage is in-built in these firms' business model and is not a financing choice. The DuPont framework quite elegantly brings out the implications of these features in the way margins, asset utilization, and financial leverage contribute to ROE.

---

[24]This is not a simple book value calculation but a present value calculation of the liabilities based on actuarial estimates.

CHAPTER 6

Revisiting the DuPont Analysis Framework

Now that we have applied the DuPont framework to different sectors and types of business models, this is a good stage to pause to assimilate and reflect upon the patterns derived from the numbers and discussions.

Certain caveats are in order before we can progress with the discussion. The metrics in Table 6.1 will be used to bring out differences across industries and their peculiarities but the seven firms used in the table cannot be categorically stated to be ideal representatives of their respective industries. This especially holds for Bhushan Steel Ltd., which was brought under bankruptcy proceedings in FY2017 and as seen in Chapter 3, had started showing signs of distress since FY2014.

Imagine an individual who has a certain amount of money that she would like to invest in the equity market. Which of the above five stocks would she prefer? Without going into future projections and outlook, prima facie she would go for HUL, the firm with the highest return on equity (ROE). An equity holder invests in a share for returns on her investment, which take the form of dividends and capital gains. An investment in the company that generates healthy returns (high ROE) for the equity holder is likely to see share price increases in the stock market too.[1] In a nutshell, an investor looking for attractive returns does not sympathize with a company or industry for its inability to generate high margins or ATR or returns. She is simply looking for high, steady returns. This means all firms in all industries are in the same race when it comes to a share of the investor's wallet.

---

[1]How ROE translates into equity value and the relationship between ROE and share price is beyond the scope of this book.

Table 6.1 *How ROE is created for shareholders across industries*

Components of ROE across industries	NOPAT margin (1) (%)	ATR (2)	ROA (3) = (1) × (2) (%)	RES (4) (%)	LEV (5)	Leverage impact (6) = (4) × (5)	ROE (7) = (2) × (6) (%)
Banking (ICICI Bank)	13.31*	0.10	1.31	NA	7.87	7.87	10.33
IT Services (TCS Ltd.)	18.79	2.22	41.70	99.86	0.67	0.67	28.02
Retail (HUL)	10.93	3.19	34.83	99.11	1.68	1.67	58.15
Heavy industry (Bhushan)	15.97	0.24	3.78	1.72	4.84	0.08	0.32
Telecom (BAL)	12.51	0.47	5.87	20.07	2.78	0.56	3.27
General insurance (ICICI Lombard)	8.93	0.37	3.31	95.95	5.81	5.58	18.44
Life Insurance (Birla Sun Life)	2.24	0.18	0.41	100	19.47	19.47	8.03

Note: All figures pertain to FY2017 except the figures for Bhushan, for which FY2014 figures have been used.
*For the banking industry NOPAT is a meaningless measure as is RES. Hence, NPM for ICICI Bank has been used in column (1). All figures include only operational metrics of each of the firms; other income, exceptional items, and nonoperating assets are excluded.

HUL's ROE is a combination of average operating margins, high asset utilization, reasonable leverage but very low interest burden resulting in very high RES. The composite impact of leverage is a healthy equity multiplier of 1.67x, which has helped amplify HUL's already impressive ROA of 34.83 percent to an enviable ROE of 58.15 percent. A retail or FMCG company that operates in a competitive industry where pricing pressure is high has to make do with moderate to low margins. Operating margins (EBIT and NOPAT) have to be managed by controlling costs and more importantly, by scaling up. Economies of scale are very important in this industry and that implies high volumes. Volumes have to be high enough to more than compensate for the competitive pricing these firms work with so that the ATR is sufficiently high to enable the firm to post a healthy ROA. FMCG and retail businesses hold high inventory and hence, have high working capital requirements, which necessitate working capital credit. While retail firms do not have manufacturing assets, FMCG firms do, and therefore need and can, afford to use financial leverage on their balance sheet, albeit moderately. Moderate to low profit margins mean that such firms have to be careful about the interest burden their operations can carry. This fine balance helps the firm to arrive at an equity multiplier that can enhance the ROA by one-half or two times for the equity holders.

A firm in the heavy industry such as iron and steel, mining, or infrastructure has features common with an FMCG firm by virtue of their manufacturing activity. Both hold significant inventory and receivables, which makes working capital an important component of the balance sheet. Therefore, both types of businesses use working capital credit that appears as part of their current liabilities. Both types of firms invest in fixed assets ranging from manufacturing assets to office assets and warehousing. However, the scale of investment in fixed assets is significantly higher in the case of heavy industries requiring a large amount of capital to be invested with relatively longer gestation periods. These factors make firms in such sectors depend on borrowings much more than a firm in the retail or FMCG sectors. The financial leverage is, therefore, higher in the heavy industries sectors.

High leverage implies higher interest burden. This requires a firm to generate huge revenues and manage healthy margins on such revenues in order that its operations are able to bear the burden of the interest expense. Huge revenues mean that assets need to be utilized well and fast translating into high ATR. Businesses engaged in mining or metals are clearly commodity based where prices are determined by the international market and product differentiation or premium pricing is not possible. Therefore, they too need to rely on high volumes to post high ATR, that is, compete in the market for share on factors other than price, unlike FMCG firms, which can engage in some premium pricing on the basis of product features, quality, and brand. Second, they need to work hard on controlling costs in order to manage margins, similar to FMCG firms. Economies of scale are of essence to the success and returns for these firms. Another crucial difference between heavy industry and FMCG firms when it comes to their cost structure is the selling and marketing expenses. FMCG firms operate in a highly competitive B2C market where margins are tight but they need to spend heavily on marketing efforts to maintain their market share and price premiums. Metal and mining firms, on the other hand, while operating in a competitive market with low margins, do not spend on similar marketing activities as they operate in a B2B space. So both sets of firms have to earn returns on their assets deployed through low to moderate margins and high asset utilization.

The crucial difference between the two sets of firms is the extent of financial leverage they employ. Heavy industry firms have to, most often, necessarily employ high financial leverage, which needs to be supported by reasonably high operating profits to carry the interest burden. This requires the firm to be able to command a good market share with prices high enough to translate into high revenues[2] and have a good grip on its business model as to control costs for efficient operations. Therefore, the number of conditions that have to play in the firm's favor is much more in the case of heavy industries than in the case of FMCG firms.

A service industry such as telecommunications resembles a metals and mining industry in many ways. They are both fixed assets intensive that

---

[2]Commodity industries follow business cycles and prices of the output also correspondingly go up and come down. During downturns most such firms see their margins touching low single digits or even going negative. Those who manage to survive this phase ride the upswings, while others may fold up. Bhushan Steel Ltd. was one of the latter that fell victim to the commodity price meltdown of the early 2010s.

have relatively long gestation periods, requiring high financial leverage to be employed. Hence, the need to generate revenues and profits high enough to carry the interest burden weighs on both sets of firms. The differences lie in the working capital composition—a telecom industry does not carry the type or scale of raw material and finished goods inventory a metals company needs to. Second, while a metals company almost necessarily plays on thin margins as price is dictated by international markets (we assume an open economy here), a telecom firm may well be playing in a monopolistic market and hence enjoying premium pricing. Of course, in a competitive setup as in India today, telecom firms are undercutting each other heavily on price through discounts and other attractions for customers. It is a tightrope balancing act between acquiring market share and managing margins. This is evident from the metrics for BAL. Tough competition and price wars have capped revenue growth and affected profit margins, bringing the interest coverage ratio precariously close to 1.0. Therefore, in terms of how they generate returns for the shareholder, both these sets of firms have to follow pretty much the same protocol.

Both BAL and TCS are service firms and therefore, carry no inventory of raw material and finished goods. The similarity ends there. An IT services firm (as contrasted with an IT products firm say, HP or Cisco) is extremely asset light, which implies that it can post high ATR far more easily than the firms above and start generating revenues almost immediately upon investing. Second, it can work with negligible or zero debt on the funding front. These provide a firm like TCS huge advantage over the manufacturing firms or even the asset-heavy service firms described above. With no material cost on the P&L statement, the largest cost component of these firms as seen earlier is employees cost, which is a semifixed cost. This is both a boon and a bane. For a firm that has high market share and raking up huge volumes, this provides economies of scale. During downturns and other economic shocks, firms have to make the difficult choice between living with lower margins and downsizing. In a reasonably healthy economy, these firms can earn attractive profit margins based on the quality of service they provide, similar to consulting firms. A high ATR and healthy margins combination automatically results in high ROA for such service industries. This "undue" advantage is evened out when it comes to financial leverage. These firms almost do not get the benefit of trading on equity, that is, the equity multiplier effect through financial leverage. On the contrary, as seen in the case of TCS, there is a real risk of the profit, cash, and equity accumulation outpacing the firm's reinvestment requirements. There is a real risk of excess equity accumulated to be parked in financial investments or deployed in suboptimal acquisitions or other investments that yield returns lower than that yielded by core operating assets. This brings down the composite return to shareholders, as the equity multiplier is less than 1.0. Having said this, technology-based industries also face fast changes in technology that need to be kept pace with and improved upon. Therefore, investment in the next big technology or service offering is becoming ever more important for these firms. Going forward, one might expect the ATR to come down as these firms will necessarily have to make significant investments in future *stars* as their *cash cows* mature.

Finally, we have the financial services that bear some resemblance to the services model such as TCS' but have certain features that are unique. With financial assets dominating their balance sheets, whether loans, advances, or investments, the ATR of financial services firms is substantially driven by and limited by the prevailing market yields. These firms are highly leveraged but not in the manner seen for nonfinancial services firms. Market borrowings are not these firms' predominant source of financial leverage. In fact, high financial leverage on the balance sheet is built into their business model and is not a matter of choice. Their key customers—whether depositors or policyholders—are also their largest creditors. Liabilities owed to them create high financial leverage for these businesses.

The ATR of ICICI Bank is barely 10 percent as lending activity dominates its business portfolio. With nonfund activities taking a larger role in banking, one may see ATRs going up in future but they still will be nowhere close to what the goods-based and asset-light service firms can notch up. Therefore, banks have to work twice as hard on their margins to post even low single-digit ROAs. Their unique business model also lends itself to almost nondiscretionary high leverage. Deposits and borrowings are a commercial bank's raw material and interest expense is its core material cost. In such a setup, the concept of interest coverage ratio (and by corollary, RES) become meaningless. The high leverage of a bank, not moderated by the factor of RES, helps amplify the ROA to high ROE for its shareholders. It certainly does not mean that a bank can take on unlimited leverage; high interest expense gets reflected right at its gross profit margin or net interest margin (NIM) levels itself.

General insurance company ICICI Lombard's numbers too look quite similar to the bank's. Leverage is high, though not as much. ATR is moderate; not as low as a bank's. An insurer earns through two primary activities—underwriting and investment. While the returns on the investment activity are driven by the yields and market movements, underwriting helps provide economies of scale and post higher ATR. Margins are tough to make in a highly competitive and commoditized general insurance industry, but efficiencies can help maintain margins in the double digits. Moderate margins and moderate ATR can get moderate ROA for a general insurer. Leverage on policyholder liabilities helps push this up to market acceptable ROE levels for the equity holder.

A life insurer's game is more complicated. While it also undertakes underwriting and investment activities, the latter takes on a larger proportion than for general insurance. This is because life insurance products very often double up as investment products too and the time horizon for such products is long-term as against event based or annual for a general insurance product. This is reflected in the phenomenally high leverage of over 19 times at Birla Sun Life. With investment activity dominating the underwriting activity at life insurers in India, one can expect ATR to be more market dependent than for general insurers, and hence lower. Similarly, margins can also be expected to be slightly lower, thereby, pushing ROA to a more humble range than for general insurance firms. Leverage is the single largest pillar on which ROE rests, similar to a bank, for life insurers. This makes their business model riskier and more fragile. With customers preferring term insurance over insurance-cum-investment products, one might expect to see metrics of life insurers come closer to general insurers' over time.

Table 6.2 summarizes the various business models in terms of the components of the DuPont framework.

Having seen some very varied business models that make returns for their shareholders through different combinations of the three levers—margins, asset productivity, and financial leverage—what are some insights we can draw about business and financial statements?

Table 6.2 Business models in terms of components of the DuPont framework

Components of ROE across industries	Profit margins	Asset utilization	Financial leverage
Retail (HUL)	Low to moderate	High	Low to moderate
Heavy industry (Bhushan)	Low	Moderate to high	High
Telecom (BAL)	Low to moderate	Moderate to high	High
IT Services (TCS Ltd.)	Moderate to High	High to very high	Very low
Banking (ICICI Bank)	Moderate	Very low	Very high
General Insurance (ICICI Lombard)	Moderate	Moderate	High
Life Insurance (Birla Sun Life)	Low to moderate	Low to moderate	Very high

In the equity market, all firms and all businesses are fighting for a slice of the investor's wallet. Hence, a business model that can combine these levers to produce competitive ROE and hence, market returns for the equity holder, has a chance at survival. The combination decides business strategy to be pursued as well as the fragility or vulnerability of the firm to external shocks. The financial statements can be mere sets of numbers in the hands of the analyst or they can be converted into a meaningful story behind the numbers!

CHAPTER 7

The Stakeholder Perspective to Financial Statements Analysis

The DuPont analysis that has largely been the focus of this book looks at financial statements from the perspective of the equity holder. This framework is not the only way to study financial statements, nor is it always required. While this is a comprehensive approach and broadly combines the lookout for all stakeholders of a firm, some stakeholders may do well to just focus on part of this framework. We will look at some key stakeholders as examples to understand how portions of this framework can be pieced out by them to suit their purposes.

DuPont Framework for the Lender

A lender is normally interested in the due servicing of his debt—timely principal repayments and timely payments of interest. Therefore, adequacy of operating profits and cash flows for regular debt servicing is what a lender is concerned with. Any profits in excess of this requirement benefits only the equity holders and lenders have no share in it. Therefore, ROE as a metric is not of much interest to lenders. Of the four elements of the DuPont framework—RES, NOPAT margin, ATR, and LEV—the one that would be of interest to them will be only RES. RES captures the extent to which EBIT earned by the firm covers its interest liabilities and hence, the buffer to afford declines in profitability and/or increase in financial leverage. Further, the *amount of* EBIT depends on the firm's ATR and its EBIT margin. So, in a sense they are interdependent.

But RES directly decides how much debt the firm can afford on its balance sheet. Another metric a lender is interested in is the cash flow from operations (CFO). While the P&L statement may show sufficient operating profits to cover interest expense, interest has to be paid in cash. Whether profits are adequately getting converted into cash is very important for the lender.

DuPont Framework for the Supplier

Similar to the lender, the supplier of material or services needs assurance of payment for goods and services rendered. As unsecured creditors, suppliers of a firm have a claim on revenues and assets after secured creditors. Therefore, they too are interested in consistent profitability and cash flows from operations in a firm and would prefer lesser financial leverage. In fact, a shorter term view would be that suppliers are interested in cash flow, whether through operations or financing, such that their dues are repaid. But a longer-term view is one where they also care about sustained business with the firm. This requires the firm to be profitable not just in the immediate period but to have such potential for the future as well.

Specifically within the DuPont framework, the elements of interest to suppliers would be ATR and EBIT. Amounts owed to suppliers normally comprise current liabilities of the firm. A healthy current ratio provides them security so long as the components of this current ratio are sufficiently liquid. At the same time, for continued business, they need these assets to generate sufficient revenues and hence, healthy ATR is also of interest to them. Further, healthy operating profit margins on this revenue are required for the firm's sustenance and growth, besides steady operating cash flows.

DuPont Framework for the Employee

What is an employee concerned about? Salary on time and conviction that the firm would not close down and leave her without a job. In that sense, an employee behaves just like a supplier and unsecured creditor. She would like to see steady growth in revenues that convert into healthy profits and cash flows. However, compensation of employees is not restricted to a fixed salary. She might have a variable pay or bonus component and may be even stock options. In this situation, her interests will be more aligned with the equity holder of the firm. Besides, an employee looks for career growth through promotions and career enhancement, which should result in higher compensation as well. An employee can grow only when the organization grows. Here again, her elements of interest would be all performance parameters similar to an equity holder.

Parting Thoughts

Accounting, and by extension financial statements, conjure up a picture of an old, wiry person cooped up in a window-less room surrounded by mountains of books, paper, and files, poring over numbers that make sense to only him! It has been seen as the domain of the accountant, his clerk, and their department. It is true that posting vouchers, passing accounting entries, and drawing up books is still the domain of the accountants and their ilk, but understanding financial statements in order to understand the underlying business is very much the business of everyone having any interest or stake in the organization. The purpose of this book has been to demystify financial statements (there are limits to which they can be demystified though!) by laying out in a simple fashion what each of these statements has to convey and how they can be read together to string a story about the business.

By now it should be clear that the financial statements are a treasure trove of information and insights. Unearthing these insights requires basic knowledge of accounting concepts, principles, and tools only (you need not necessarily know how to draw up a journal or a ledger) and of the business of the firm being analyzed. It also requires reading the numbers along with qualitative information provided by the management and of course, reading between the lines. Most important, financial statement analysis is only as good as, first, the inputs available, that is, the quality and veracity of the financial statements and accompanying information, and second, as the skill of the analyst. The person(s) and purpose for which financial statements are being studied should drive the analysis; there is no one-size-fits-all method or approach to financial analysis.

I sincerely hope this primer has been useful to the reader, especially to one who started with limited knowledge of financial accounting and statements. Most executives who hold top management positions in companies either as heads of businesses or functions, have a fair to very good understanding of their business. However, this knowledge remains incomplete so long as they are unable to sync the numbers in the annual report to such understanding and at the same time unable to translate their business decisions into implications for financial statements.

References

Alchian, A., and H. Demsetz. 1972. "Production, Information Costs and Economic Organization." *The American Economic Review* 62, no. 5, pp. 777–795.

Coase, R. 1937. "The Nature of the Firm." *Economica* 4, no. 16, pp. 386–405.

Jensen, M.C., and W.H. Meckling. 1976. "Theory of the Firm: Managerial Behavior, Agency Costs and Ownership Structure." *Journal of Financial Economics* 3, no. 4, p. 78.

Miller, M.H., 1995, "Do the M&M propositions apply to banks?", *Journal of Banking & Finance*, no. 19, p. 483–489.

Mulford, C.W., and E. Comiskey. 2009. *Cash Flow Reporting by Financial Companies: A look at the commercial banks.* Atlanta, GA: College of Management, Georgia Institute of Management.

Torfason, A. 2014. "Cash flow accounting in banks: A study of practice." Doctoral thesis. University of Gothenburg, Gothenburg, Sweden.

Glossary

List of Financial Terms

Acronym	Expanded form	Definition/explanatory note
"kd"	Cost of debt	Average cost of debt, measured as interest expense divided by average debt outstanding in a period
"t"	Income tax rate	Average tax rate applicable to the firm, measured as Tax provision divided by pretax profit for the period
ATR	Asset turnover ratio	Measures how well assets are utilized, calculated as revenues for the period divided by average operating assets employed. Higher the ratio, better is asset utilization.
Capex	Capital expenditure	Investment in long-term operating assets during a period, this is recorded in the cash flow statement
C-D ratio	Credit-to-deposits ratio	Ratio of loans and advances outstanding to deposits held by a lending institution at a point in time, it has implications for credit generation and profitability of banking operations
CFF	Cash flows from financing activities	One of the three buckets of the CFS, it describes the cash flows on account of financing activities undertaken by a firm during the accounting period
CFI	Cash flows from investment activities	One of the three buckets of the CFS, it describes the cash flows on account of investments and divestments in long-term assets undertaken by a firm during the accounting period
CFO	Cash flows from operations	One of the three buckets of the CFS, it describes the cash flows on account of operations undertaken by a firm during the accounting period
CFS	Cash flow statement	One of the principal financial statements that informs about the movement of cash during the accounting period

Acronym	Expanded form	Definition/explanatory note
CRAR	Capital to risk-weighted assets ratio	Also referred to as "capital adequacy ratio," it is a measure of the equity buffer a lending institution keeps in relation to its risky assets (typically loans, investments and commitments). Higher the ratio, greater is the equity buffer and ability to withstand shocks to the balance sheet.
D/E	Debt to equity ratio	Long-term debt divided by shareholder funds, it is a common measure of financial indebtedness of a firm. Higher the ratio, higher is financial leverage employed.
DSCR	Debt service coverage ratio	Measures the extent to which operating profits cover debt servicing commitments for the accounting period; computed as EBITDA divided by interest, principal installments and lease payments falling due during the period. Higher the ratio, higher is the cover and lesser is the risk of default by the firm.
EBIT	Earnings before interest and taxes	Profits from core operations a firm engages in
EBITDA	Earnings before interest, taxes, depreciation and amortization	Also referred to as "cash operating profits," it is the profits from core operations before providing for depreciation and amortization on assets
FCF	Free cash flows	Computed as after-tax profits plus depreciation and amortization charges less capex, it indicates the amount of cash flow remaining for equity-holders after reinvestment needs of the firm have been taken care of
GNPA	Gross nonperforming assets	Akin to bad and doubtful debts in other firms, this is the total loans and advances made by lending institutions that have defaulted on interest and/or principal payments
HTM	Held-to-maturity investments	Financial investments by firms with an intent to not trade but to hold them until maturity to be redeemed at predetermined redemption values. These are therefore, not marked to market.
ICR	Interest coverage ratio	Computed as EBIT (or sometimes EBITDA) divided by interest expenses for the period, it indicates the number of times operating profits "cover" the interest expenses for the period. Higher the ratio, higher is the cover and lower is default risk by the firm.

Acronym	Expanded form	Definition/explanatory note
I-D ratio	Investments-to-deposits ratio	Ratio of investments held to deposits held by a lending institution at a point in time, it has implications for credit generation and profitability of banking operations
LEV	Financial leverage	Measured as average assets divided by average equity over a period, it is an indicator of financial leverage employed by a firm. Higher the ratio, higher is the financial leverage.
MtM	Marked-to-market	Financial investments held by firms for trading (not HTM) are marked to market at regular intervals to reflect notional gains/ losses due to movement in their market prices.
NIM	Net interest margin	One of the key operating metrics for lending institutions, it is calculated as difference in interest income and interest expenses divided by average interest earning assets over a period.
NNPA	Net nonperforming assets	They are GNPA that have not been provided for in the balance sheet of a lending institution from profits of prior and/ or current periods.
NOPAT	Net operating profits after taxes	Computed as EBIT multiplied by (1-tax rate), it is the post-tax operating profits that would accrue to a firm not considering impact of interest expenses.
NPM	Net profits margin	Measured as profits after tax divided by revenues for the period, it indicates the percentage of revenues remaining for equity holders after dues toward all other stakeholders has been provided for.
NWC	Net working capital	Computed as current assets less current liabilities, it indicates the extent to which current assets are funded by long-term noncurrent sources of funding
OI	Other income	Incomes/ revenues earned by firms from noncore activities or incidental activities. Such income should account for a trivial proportion of the firm's overall revenues.
P&L	Profit and loss statement	One of the principal financial statements that informs about the revenues, expenses and hence, profit and loss earned during an accounting period.

Acronym	Expanded form	Definition/explanatory note
PAT	Profits after taxes	Also called net income, it indicates the residual of revenues remaining for equity holders after dues toward all other stakeholders has been provided for.
PBT	Profits before taxes	The last set of dues a firm has is to the state, in the form of taxes. PBT is the profits remaining after all other dues but taxes have been provided for.
PCR	Provisioning coverage ratio	Computed as provisions divided by GNPA as at a date, it indicates the extent to which GNPA have been provided for; the unprovided portion of GNPA is NNPA.
RES	(Measure of) Resilience	Not a standard financial ratio, RES is measured as (1 - 1/ICR) and indicates the extent to cushion the firm's profits provide for affording volatility in operations and increasing debts without causing financial distress.
ROA	Return on assets	Measured as EBIT (or NOPAT) divided by average assets, it is a comprehensive measure of the returns generated on assets employed over the period.
ROE	Return on equity	Measured as PAT divided by average shareholder equity, it is a comprehensive measure of the returns provided by a firm to its equity-holders over the period.
ROIC	Return on invested capital	Measured as EBIT (or NOPAT) divided by average capital employed (long term liabilities + shareholder equity), it is a comprehensive measure of the returns provided by a firm to long-term fund providers over the period.
RONW	Return on net worth	It is another term for return on equity
RWA	Risk weighted assets	When assets of lending institutions are assigned weights based on their estimated riskiness, the sum total is called RWA. This is used in the computation of capital adequacy ratio.

List of General Terms

Acronym	Expanded form	Definition/explanatory note
B2B	Business-to-Business	Firms that serve other businesses
B2C	Business-to-Consumer	Firms that serve retail consumers
BAL	Bharti Airtel Limited	A leading telecommunications company in India
FMCG	Fast moving consumer goods	Industry classification for nondurable, short-lived products, e.g. toiletries, packaged food.
FY	Financial year	Most Indian companies follow an April to March financial year as their annual accounting period.
HUL	Hindustan Unilever Limited	The Indian subsidiary of Unilever Plc., HUL is one of the largest FMCG firms in India.
IFRS	International Financial Reporting Standards	A set of international accounting standards stating how particular types of transactions and other events should be reported in financial statements, IFRS are issued by the International Accounting Standards Board (IASB), Europe.
INR	Indian Rupees	Legal tender used in India
MHz	Mega Hertz (a measure of frequency of sound)	
RBI	Reserve Bank of India	Central bank of India, RBI is the banking industry regulator and the supreme monetary authority in the country.
RIL	Reliance Industries Limited	A leading conglomerate in India that engages in businesses from retail to oil exploration, refining and retailing.
TCS	Tata Consultancy Services	One of India's leading information technology services companies
U.S. GAAP	U.S. Generally Accepted Accounting Practices	Accounting standards followed in the U.S.A, set by the American Institute of Certified Public Accountants (AICPA)

About the Author

Dr. S. Veena Iyer is assistant professor of accounting and finance at the Management Development Institute, Gurgaon, India. She teaches financial accounting, business valuation, and management of financial services businesses to management students at the postgraduate level. She holds a masters in business economics from the University of Delhi and is a fellow of the Indian Institute of Management, Bangalore. She has more than a decade of experience in the corporate sector leading teams of analysts engaged in business and management research on client projects.

Index

OTHER TITLES IN OUR FINANCIAL ACCOUNTING AND AUDITING COLLECTION

Mark Bettner, Bucknell University and
Michael Coyne, Fairfield University, *Editors*

- *Accounting History and the Rise of Civilization, Volume I* by Gary Giroux
- *Accounting History and the Rise of Civilization, Volume II* by Gary Giroux
- *A Refresher in Financial Accounting* by Faisal Sheikh
- *Accounting Fraud, Second Edition: Maneuvering and Manipulation, Past and Present* by Gary Giroux
- *Corporate Governance in the Aftermath of the Global Financial Crisis, Volume I: Relevance and Reforms* by Zabihollah Rezaee
- *Corporate Governance in the Aftermath of the Global Financial Crisis, Volume II: Functions and Sustainability* by Zabihollah Rezaee
- *Corporate Governance in the Aftermath of the Global Financial Crisis, Volume III: Gatekeeper Functions* by Zabihollah Rezaee
- *Corporate Governance in the Aftermath of the Global Financial Crisis, Volume IV: Emerging Issues in Corporate Governance* by Zabihollah Rezaee
- *Using Accounting & Financial Information, Second Edition: Analyzing, Forecasting, and Decision Making* by Mark S. Bettner
- *Pick a Number, Second Edition: The U.S. and International Accounting* by Roger Hussey

Announcing the Business Expert Press Digital Library

Concise e-books business students need for classroom and research

This book can also be purchased in an e-book collection by your library as

- *a one-time purchase,*
- *that is owned forever,*
- *allows for simultaneous readers,*
- *has no restrictions on printing, and*
- *can be downloaded as PDFs from within the library community.*

Our digital library collections are a great solution to beat the rising cost of textbooks. E-books can be loaded into their course management systems or onto students' e-book readers.
The **Business Expert Press** digital libraries are very affordable, with no obligation to buy in future years. For more information, please visit **www.businessexpertpress.com/librarians**.
To set up a trial in the United States, please email **sales@businessexpertpress.com**.

CPSIA information can be obtained
at www.ICGtesting.com
Printed in the USA
FFHW012004010819
53997710-59734FF

9 781947 843769